W9-DBJ-663

OVER
OUR
LIVE
BODIES

PRESERVING CHOICE
IN AMERICA

SHIRLEY L. RADL

Foreword by CYBILL SHEPHERD

STEVE DAVIS PUBLISHING
Dallas, Texas

Sponsored by
The California Pro-Choice Education Fund,
Educational Affiliate of the
California Abortion Rights Action League

A Quality of Life Book

Published by
STEVE DAVIS PUBLISHING
Dallas, Texas

Cover design by Gary DiGiovanni

ISBN 0-911061-20-7
Library of Congress Catalog Card Number 89-51215

Additional copies of this book are available for $7.95, plus
$1.50 postage for the first book and 50 cents postage for each
additional book. Send a check or money order, or provide your
Visa, Mastercard, American Express or Discover card number
with expiration date and phone number. Send your order to:

STEVE DAVIS PUBLISHING
P.O. Box 190831
Dallas, Texas 75219

Special discounts are available for bulk purchases by
organizations for fund-raising and educational use.

Table of Contents

Acknowledgments

My first thanks must go to Cari Beauchamp, Chair of the California Abortion Rights Action League, and Pat Miller, Chair of the California Pro-Choice Education Fund. Without their inspiration and wonderful support, this book would never have been possible.

Merloyd Lawrence generously contributed both time and money to this project to make it possible for me to complete the work. Words are inadequate to express my gratitude for the confidence she inspired in me.

The same holds true for Steve Davis, whose publishing house is small, but who eagerly decided to take an enormous financial risk in publishing this book. Steve made a commitment that few publishers would have made. He gave the book his full attention to make it available to the public as quickly as possible.

There is no way I can adequately thank my husband, Cal Radl, for his contribution to this effort. Most authors who acknowledge the role their spouses played in bringing any work to fruition talk about the moral support that was lent during the writing. Well, there was that, to be sure. But, there was much more: Cal pitched in and helped with proofreading, editing, making corrections, and participating in this very first desk-top publishing effort. I may have written this book, but together, we created it with all four of our hands.

I am deeply indebted to Diana Workman, President of Family Planning Alternatives (FPA), and to Carol

Chetkovich, my long-time friend and Vice Chair of FPA. Diana made many suggestions to make the book better, and Carol, going far beyond the call of duty, devoted precious hours to line-editing the manuscript. Another who went well beyond the call is Sarah Weddington. When she was asked to read the book and possibly make a comment, not only did she put on her lawyer's hat and clarify legal points, but she put on her English teacher's hat and made many suggestions for clarifying the book as a whole. I thank her for taking the time to help me make this a better book.

I am also indebted to Regina Garrick for compiling a bibliography on the history of choice that served as a foundation for my research. And I'm grateful to Jerrie Meadows, past Chair of the California Pro-Choice Education Fund, for taking the time to read the manuscript and give it her blessings. I'm grateful to Jerrie too for putting me in touch with Sherry Matulis whose moving piece about her own experience is included in the first chapter of this book. And, of course, thanks to Sherry for allowing me to reproduce it here.

Finally, I would like to thank Cybill Shepherd for generously gracing this small volume with the next words you will read.

Foreword

Why is this book important? We stand at a paradoxical crossroad in the history of women's rights in America. Women have enjoyed greater reproductive freedom of choice for the past 16 years; however, this freedom is in danger of being taken away. This book explains how this situation developed and the specific threats that are currently being leveled against the fundamental right of privacy to choose one's reproductive path.

This book traces our recent history from back-alley abortions to the movement to provide safe, legal abortion. It raises many important questions. We need to know the answers, not only because *Roe v. Wade* is in danger of being overturned, but also because of the dangerous trend toward limiting access to abortions. When safe, legal abortions become restricted, who will suffer? Poor women. The women without the money to travel to a state where there is access to safe and legal abortion.

But there is hope. The anti-choice faction represents a minority view. A clear majority of all Americans, while understanding the personal moral dilemma, favor choice. If that majority stops being a silent one, the trend toward state intervention into our personal freedom can be halted.

Cybill Shepherd
Voters for Choice

Chapter 1

THE WAY THINGS WERE

> You see...the issue never really had much to do with legality or illegality. It had to do with economics...those who could afford it would be off to London or Puerto Rico or Mexico, although even there they'd sometimes run into shabby practices. Or they'd be someone helped by their own doctors to get into a hospital here...Or sometimes another out would be finding and paying psychiatrists to swear she was suicidal; she would jump out the window if the pregnancy continued. And of course in some instances that was absolutely true, and in some instances it wasn't...it was very soon obvious to me that the fundamental issue here about abortion was never legality or illegality but basically whom you knew and how much you could pay.
>
> Dr. Moshe Hachamovitch
> East Medical Group
> in *Moments on Maple Avenue*, 1984

The year was 1929. My mother, a Roman Catholic of Irish descent, had had two babies, eleven months apart. As she explained it, one minute she had been a happy wife and mother married to a hard-working plasterer and carpenter, and seemingly the next, my father was out of work. The depression had hit full force and had taken with it the building trades in California. For weeks, my father looked in vain for work and watched their small savings account vanish to put food on the table and pay the rent. As the finance company repossessed the last stick of furniture, my father got a letter from a friend saying there was work in Reno. With high hopes, he and my mother bundled up their small children, climbed into their last remaining possession, their rattletrap car, and left their native San Francisco.

The "work in Reno" turned out to be a caretaking job and a maid's job for a wealthy Reno woman in exchange for an unheated one-room cottage set at the back of the estate. Food was another matter, so my father would go into town and offer his services as a gardener, janitor, wood-chopper, carpenter, whatever, and most days he would earn just enough to keep his young family from starvation.

For a time, even through snowy weather, they managed to keep from freezing to death; father found and installed an old wood stove in the cottage and would chop wood to keep it going at all times. As for warming their hearts, this nice young couple soon made many friends, mostly people who were similarly down on their luck.

After a few months of my mother keeping a spotless house for the wealthy woman and my father doing his caretaking and odd jobs, my mother discovered that she was pregnant. She went into a blind panic. They could barely feed the two children they had; no way could they stretch their resources to feed one more mouth. Worse was a deep and abiding fear that their employer would see my mother's pregnancy as a burden, to say nothing of one more child on the premises, and put the family out on the street. One of my parents' friends knew of "someone who could help"; another offered to throw ten hard-earned dollars into the pot; another offered two, and another five, and another and another until they got together the amount they would need.

At the appointed time, my petite mother, not quite twenty-five years of age and not quite one hundred pounds, accompanied by my twenty-six-year-old father, went to the designated dark street corner. There, my mother was blindfolded, told to turn over the money, and guided into the back seat of a car, while my father was pushed aside as he tried to slide into the seat beside her.

My mother traveled with the gruff stranger for an hour or more. Not a word was spoken. She was terrified beyond words. Finally, the car came to a stop and she was led up seven or eight rickety wooden stairs. She thought she might be at a farmhouse somewhere on the outskirts of Reno. When her blindfold was removed, she found herself standing in the middle of a filthy kitchen. The "doctor" instructed her to get onto the kitchen table and spread her legs. She obeyed. Without an anesthetic, he went to work with "his knives, carving my insides out." The next thing my mother remembered was being back in her own bed in the cottage and waking up to see and hear giant cockroaches "the size of German shepherd dogs, crawling all around the room." Hallucinating and hemorrhaging she struggled to take care of her already-born children.

When she told me the story in the late 1960's, she said that she had no regrets. She had, after all, survived the ordeal, and as she explained, "I had an obligation to the children I already had. What else could I have done?"

There had never been any question about *wanting* more children, and later on, when they were no longer dirt poor, my parents had two more, my brother and me. But, they were determined, especially my mother, not to bring children into the world with no way to care for them. Like many women throughout history, she was driven by an inner determination that found her risking her very life.

That was, she said, the way it was in 1929.

And that was the way it was in 1939. And in 1949, 1959, and 1969. And all of the years in all of those decades for women without wealth or connections.

In 1946, a woman I know, who is now sixty years old, discovered that she was pregnant. She was not an impoverished, depression-years married woman worried to death that she could not feed the children she already had. She was, instead, a frightened teenager who had made a "mistake." She had let her steady boyfriend "have his way with her." Even though he may have forced the issue, the "sin" was hers, for in those good old days, it was thought that "boys will be boys" and they will always try to go as far as they can. It was up to the girls—the "weaker sex"—to draw the line. Even if the boy had *raped* the girl, it would have been thought to be her fault, as she had somehow either brought it on herself or had not fought hard enough to avoid the ultimate act.

And, if she got pregnant and that became obvious, her "sin" quite literally showed itself. If she was lucky, and her boyfriend was a decent sort, a girl in "such a fix" could get married at fifteen, be a mother at sixteen, and be forever stigmatized for "having had to get married." Other options included going to a home for unwed mothers, the coat hanger, or the back-alley abortionist.

Terrified, and wanting only to put her life back together, my friend "knew someone who knew someone." She managed to get together the several hundred dollars required, and went for the blindfold and the excursion to the country. The scene and the experience she described were nearly identical to the horrors my mother had spoken of. But, like my mother, she had no regrets: "It would have been impossible for me to continue the pregnancy," she told me. "It just wasn't done back then. My life would have been over. I was terrified. It was horrible, but, given the same circumstances I'd do it again."

Two decades later that saw many changes in American society, the song remained the same where freedom of choice was concerned. In 1965, another woman I know crossed the border from California to Tijuana to obtain an abortion. When it was over, she was cast out of the clinic and, as she made her way across the border back into California, she collapsed, hemorrhaging. At roughly the same time, a woman friend told me of a friend of hers, a twenty-one-year old English woman, a graduate student at Stanford University who made the same south-of-the-border trip and was less fortunate. The promising young scientist died at Stanford Hospital two weeks after the abortion. "I couldn't believe it," my friend told me. "One moment this bright 21-year-old was vibrantly alive, looking forward to getting her degree, and the next thing I knew she was dead. There had been complications, I was told, from an illegal abortion."

As an aside, I have often wondered how the heartbroken parents of the young woman from England might have felt about having sent their daughter to a "free" country whose laws had imposed a death sentence upon her.

A woman I spoke with, who is now in her fifties and who will never have to confront making a choice on a personal level, is very active in the pro-choice movement. Ask her why and you will hear a familiar story of a young, frightened teenager who hadn't planned to have sex with her boyfriend and never expected to get pregnant when "it just happened." She will also tell you about the brutal, botched abortion that left her sterile, forever destroying her dreams of a future family.

It is anyone's guess how many women may have endured excruciating pain, humiliation, and even complications that threatened their fertility or their very lives. It is also anyone's guess how many women were driven to seek illegal abortions or attempt to perform them on themselves because they became pregnant as a result of rape or incest. Remember, nice girls never got raped in those good old days.

One who did is Sherry Matulis, who told this sordid story in 1983:

I was twenty-three, pleasantly married, the mother of two planned-for and well-loved children (the number later grew to five) and working nights....One night, I got off the 1:20 a.m. bus and started my usual trudge home, cutting the three blocks to two and one-half by what we called the schoolyard shortcut.

He must have been waiting close to the building, in the shadows. I didn't see him until he was on top of me, and I still remember very little about the act itself, not because I'm trying not to any longer, but because when he threw me down on the blacktop, my skull cracked and I blacked out.

The back of my head was sticky-wet. Blood. Lots of it. Most of my clothing had been torn off and scattered. And as I tried to retrieve it, I felt a terrible searing pain in my midsection. Like a knife I thought. Looking down, I saw this odd, ugly mass of something perched atop my abdomen. It took at least a minute to realize that it was part of my intestine. The knife was no longer there, but it had been, and my guts were oozing out of a neat X.

Holding both hands against something I hope never to feel again in my life, somehow I managed to get up; somehow I managed to get home; and somehow, with a lot of suturing and a couple of weeks' intensive care and an infinite amount of love from a husband who rushed home from three states away and never left again, I managed to survive. Only to find myself wishing, about a month later, that I hadn't.

I was pregnant. And I was not *pregnant by my husband. I was pregnant by that fiend. And I could not stay that way.*

My doctor would not help me, so I feigned migraine to get a prescription for ergotrate, which I think gave me a migraine. I went on a two-day castor-oil diet and lost five pounds and a quart of hemorrhoidal blood, and nothing else. I scalded the lower two-thirds of my anatomy squatting in hot tubs. I detested the taste of alcohol, but I held my nose and downed two pints of Everclear. And when I woke up, everything intact, I got out the meat mallet and began pounding my almost-healed abdomen.

My husband was ready to stick me in a straightjacket. He wanted me to go through with the pregnancy—or rather, he wanted me not to kill myself, or to be killed by the only sort of abortionist that was available at the time. He thought that once the baby was born, we could both accept it as our own. And good person that he is, he probably would have tried.

But I could not, not ever. I knew that had I given birth to a child conceived under those circumstances, I would not be able to look at it without remembering. And remembering would mean hating all over again. And I wasn't willing to put myself or a child through that.

When I was finally able to make him understand this, my husband reluctantly agreed to take me to the local back-alley abortionist—an alcoholic quack who buried more than one of his mistakes. This was in 1954, when a dollar was worth perhaps three times what it is today. I had to hand this drunken butcher one thousand of them before I even got through the door.

After I had swallowed my two-aspirin "anesthetic," I was told to climb up on what resembled a dirty kitchen table and hoist up my skirt. There followed a few obscene comments about my underpants and how I could take 'em off now, but I should have—ha! ha!—left 'em on before. Then the pain. Eyeball popping pain. Lots and lots of it. Far more, I'm sure than was necessary. After the... procedure was over, he offered me twenty of my one thousand bucks back for a quick blow job.

Another trip to the hospital, another ten-day stay, a little bout with peritonitis, a half-dozen transfusions (all of which we could ill afford and put me back to square one when it came to owning my own home) and the old girl was as good as new. Almost—but not quite. Not in the sense that "good" is docile or tractable or pliant or amenable or submissive or for one second willing to sit silently by while anyone tries to bring back the back-alley quack, the one they'll never have to patronize—not because they don't have abortions but because they do have pull.

In 1968, just five years before the United States Supreme Court struck down all restrictive abortion laws in the nation, Dalia Krascoff, a forty-three-year old married mother of three living children experienced the way things were. In a courageous and heartbreaking account (*San Jose Mercury News*, January 22, 1989), she shared her story, excerpted here:

When I discovered I was pregnant I experienced a faint flicker of the euphoria my husband and I had known each time we learned we had created new life together. Then the heavy sorrow of reality quickly checked that natural springing of joy. How could I carry and raise another child after burying our firstborn who succumbed to leukemia at the age of 16?

When a few well-meaning friends advised that having another baby would give the Krascoffs even more reason to go on, Dalia Krascoff said flatly, "There can be no substitutes." Moreover, she feared that another baby would send her over the edge, leaving her three daughters with, as she put it, "less of a mother than they had." Even though she had been able to force herself to go through the motions of caring for her family, she writes, "my heart was missing in all that I did." Her daughters, she felt, perceived it and felt deprived. Krascoff's one hope was that she could pick up the pieces of her life and restore some quality to parenting the children she already had. Then, she would be somewhat comforted, for "there was no spirit or stamina for starting anew."

With the decision made, the Krascoffs turned to the obstetrician who had delivered their children. He sympathized with them, but explained, "The law is the law." Next, they appealed to the counselor who was helping them work through the raw grief of having lost their son. While he was in a position to recommend therapeutic abortion because of the fragile state of Dalia Krascoff's emotional health, after listening in "stony silence," he said, "I can't risk getting involved. I could lose my license for that." Abandoned and shaken, she writes, "we realized there was no hope of hospital safety. We would be forced to turn to back-alley help and, despite its risks, be glad to get it."

From this point, Dalia Krascoff and her husband made contact through Clergy Counseling Service for Problem Pregnancies, an outfit that worked with local free clinics, directing women to doctors and clinics in various parts of the country. In this instance, the Krascoffs were dispatched to El Paso, Texas. While Dalia Krascoff was not blindfolded and whisked away as my mother was, she nonetheless became involved in what was a clandestine operation with the usual trappings: waiting long hours, and forced to endure the experience without the support of her husband who was instructed to wait it all out at a motel. The abortion itself, while antiseptic, was performed in a hastily set up treatment room, and an air of anxiety prevailed among the staff for fear of discovery. Krascoff herself was "on edge, listening for the sound of police breaking in." Writing her piece for publication on the sixteenth anniversary of *Roe v. Wade*, she laments:

When in time, the Supreme Court ruled that abortion is a private matter, I thought wistfully, why couldn't it have been in time for me? But change has come in time for my daughters' generation. The old parental dream of wanting things better for your offspring has been fulfilled.

In the 1987 movie, *Dirty Dancing*, all of the action takes place at a summer resort patterned after those vacation spots that were popular with upper-middle-class families in the fifties and sixties. Recreation and entertainment is planned and provided by the resort staff and consists of structured sports activities by day and "night-club" type entertainment in the evening, At this particular resort, for the guests' entertainment, there is a dance team, a young man and a young woman, who lead the guests with their exhibition dancing. They also earn their livelihood by appearing at surrounding clubs. When the young woman, Penny, discovers that her affair with one of the preppie-type guests has resulted in a pregnancy, for which her lover refuses to assume any responsibility, she makes arrangements to see the "doctor" who offers his clandestine services every Thursday when he comes into the area.

In the next scene, we see Penny back in her room, writhing on her bed and sobbing in apparent excruciating pain. As the friend who'd gone with her to the abortionist explains to her dancing partner and several others, the doctor wasn't a real doctor at all; he didn't give her an anesthetic and he'd used "a dirty knife."

Illustrating the lack of awareness that choice has not always been a given, my 22-year-old son turned to me and said, "I don't understand this. Why didn't Penny just go to her doctor or to a clinic?" When I explained that abortion was illegal back then and Penny didn't have such choices, he was stunned: "You mean to tell me," he said in utter disbelief, "that's the way it was when you were young?"

I started to say yes, and then I caught myself, and modified my answer. "Yes," I told him, "that's the way it was back then. But not for everybody." I remembered that in the year of his birth, 1966, *I* would have had options different from those of my own mother. I remembered sitting in my kitchen with my two babies born less than a year apart, visiting with a friend who'd come by with her baby. My friend, a member of a well-to-do and well-connected family, said to me, "If you get pregnant again, my uncle Mort [he was a gynecologist] will take care of it for you."

The laws notwithstanding, freedom of choice has been an option that women could exercise in varying degrees depending upon their economic status, level of awareness of what has been available at any given time, and who they happened to know. Had Sherry Matulis traveled in a social circle that included a number of health-care practitioners, for her one thousand dollars, it is possible she could have had a simple D&C. This is what one woman I know did that same year. Like my friend, she happened to have an uncle who was an ob/gyn on staff at a local hospital. As she tells it:

I was single and living alone in a cottage on an estate. One night this monster broke into my house and held a lead pipe over my head. I do not know how I had the presence of mind to do so, but I told him, "If you don't hurt me, I won't struggle." He raped me repeatedly and then, miraculously left without beating me with that lead pipe. Instead of calling the police—because in those days, there was this attitude that if you got raped, you asked for it—I called my uncle. He came immediately, took me to the hospital, and performed a D&C. As he told me, "As a precaution."

Another woman, the mother of three children, had an accidental fourth pregnancy. As she explained it,

I could barely cope with the three I already had. I absolutely could not handle even the thought of having another baby. My doctor was a compassionate man and a family friend. He put me in the hospital and performed

a procedure. The record showed that I'd had an appendectomy.

Other women, able to afford it, have reported traveling to Sweden, Japan, Puerto Rico, and Mexico, when they had no similar connections at home, but were able to pay for a trip and services outside the United States.

Louise Kapp Howe offers a well-documented sampling of studies on the prevalence of illegal abortion. One 1936 study, she says, estimates that 500,000 abortions were performed in the United States; at first glance, this estimate may seem high, but it must be remembered that the birth rate during the 1930's was at an all-time low, despite the lack of effective contraception (Jones, 1980).

One 1955 study cited by Howe suggests that somewhere between 200,000 and 1,200,000 illegal abortions were performed annually; four independent studies conducted in 1964 put the figure at one million.

Estimating the actual numbers of illegal abortions is tricky for the obvious reason that unless complications resulted in a visit to the hospital or the morgue, most were not reported. But one 1940 study reported that 1,682 women died from illegal abortions that year.

Whatever the actual numbers, buried within them is the irrefutable fact that in the United States, before the laws came tumbling down and the clinics started going up, the more impoverished the woman's circumstance, the greater the risk.

As Lucinda Cisler observed in 1969:

Who are the American women who die? As one might expect, they are usually the poor, the uninformed, the black, and the Spanish-speaking women: in a recent three-year period, 79 percent of New York City's abortion deaths occurred among black and Puerto Rican women; the abortion death rate was 4.7 times as high for Puerto Rican women, and eight times as high for black women, as for their white sisters. It is obvious that poor women have no access to information about legal or safe illegal abortion sources, to friendly doctors who do abortions, or to the money to pay the exorbitant charges involved....

Chapter 2

A BRIEF HISTORY OF CHOICE

Not all fertilized eggs grow into babies, and some tumors have several of the characteristics of fertilized eggs. Moreover, all through early development, there is a selective elimination of developmental errors. As few as 60 percent of early embryos survive to implantation. And perhaps fewer than half of these make it to the second week of pregnancy. More than half of a woman's conceptions may end before she is even aware of being pregnant. A substantial proportion of miscarriages involve defective embryos.

Dr. Malcolm Potts
Science '82

Abortion is not always the best alternative to an unintended pregnancy: it should never be considered the only alternative. But for some women, in some cases, it means nothing short of survival.

Diana Workman
Political Woman, 1986

Women in all lands and all ages have instinctively desired family limitation.

Margaret Sanger
Margaret Sanger: An Autobiography, 1938

From the dawn of civilization, women have recognized nature's fallibility when it comes to conception and birth and, accordingly, have devised ways to compensate for it. Nature works randomly, and even though it often compensates for its mistakes by ending a conception that shouldn't have been or has gone awry, it cannot know, as living women historically have, when a conception may threaten a woman's physical health, the well-being of the family, or the population balance of a tribe or community.

In a thorough examination of the matter, Autumn Stanley (in *The Mothers of Invention*; in press) offers indisputable evidence that women, before men, made the connection between sexual relations and conception, felt compelled to control their own fertility, and found ways to do so. Women knew, for example, that nature, fallible as it sometimes is, provided contraception for nursing mothers. So, often to limit their family size, women in early tribes nursed their young for months and years beyond the time when such was necessary to provide nourishment. They also knew that this natural contraception sometimes failed. Their survival instincts spawned resourcefulness in finding other means to control their own fertility.

As Stanley reports, in the course of devising food preparation, women discovered, sometimes quite accidentally, one plant or another would cause a spontaneous abortion in a pregnant woman. Through trial and error, they would then develop an effective dosage and application to prevent conception or to prevent a fertilized egg from attaching itself to the womb.

Aside from family or community concerns, fertility control has long been a very real survival issue for women. First, there is the fact that childbirth itself has always carried with it certain risks. Next, having many children has always been known to take a physical toll on a woman. Finally, pregnancy could be taken as evidence of adulterous conduct, an offense punishable by death in some cultures.

A Brief History of Fertility Control

A look at the early history of birth control and some of the methods women employed, before more recent medical technology gave us condoms, IUDs, the diaphragm, and the Pill, illustrates the lengths to which women historically have gone to control their fertility.

To give you an idea of how long women have been so inclined, scholar John T. Noonan says that "the existence of birth control techniques in the pre-Christian Mediterranean world is well established." He cites ancient Egyptian documents that date from between 1900 and 1100 B.C. that contain a whole roster of contraceptive recipes: pulverized crocodile dung in fermented mucilage sprinkled in the vulva; acacia tips, colquintida, and dates mixed with honey inserted in the uterus; crocodile dung with some fibers inserted in the uterus; fumigation of the uterus with the seed of a particular grain; pessaries made of all manner of material; poisonous concoctions brewed from a variety of toxic plants, ingested either to prevent pregnancy or to bring on an abortion.

In the Roman Empire, says Noonan, abortion and infanticide were widely practiced, and contraception included the use of a pessary (diaphragm), *coitus interruptus*, and various medicines and potions thought to prevent conception or induce abortion. Finally, in these early societies, there was magic: the wearing of amulets, including some made of asparagus or heliotrope, the tooth of a child, a worm from a marble quarry, to name just a few. Whether effective, dangerous, or approved by the culture, the practices speak to a very basic need. Noonan notes, "The desire to prevent pregnancy by artificial means will be found even more characteristic of the society Christians knew."

As for accessibility to the means to do so, Noonan tells us, "The impression remains that the knowledge of the variety of precise techniques...would have been the prerogative of the rich. Others would have had to depend on information passed by word of mouth, folk custom, and popular superstition."

Abortion in the New World

With variations on old themes, the actual technology of contraception and abortion as practiced by women remained relatively unchanged for centuries and, in the early days of this nation, those old methods were commonplace. Some variations included throwing oneself down a staircase, inserting objects such as knitting needles into the uterus, and risking one's health working in paint factories because it was believed that exposure to lead could cause sterility or a spontaneous abortion (Stanley).

Safe or not, for centuries, there were no specific bans against contraception or abortion in the West. Even the Catholic Church took no official position as long as it was done prior to "quickening" or when a pregnant woman could feel the fetus move (roughly between the fourth and fifth months).

Blatant advertisements for abortion and abortificients (substances thought to cause a miscarriage) regularly appeared in popular publications. So did lists of do's and don'ts to prevent miscarriages, which of course suggested ways for women to bring them about: steaming hot baths, the use of laxatives, horseback riding, and lifting heavy objects, to name a few.

Then, in 1821, in the state of Connecticut, the first law that specifically banned the practice of abortion was passed, ostensibly to protect women against dangerous procedures. Following passage of this law, a state-by-state campaign to ban abortion was launched by local physicians (again under the guise of protecting women against unsafe practices). According to historian James C. Mohr, however, physicians were largely motivated to protect their own practices from the growing competition of midwives and other "irregulars" whom they felt were encroaching on their business, presumably the business of delivering babies.

Thus, little by little there came a build-up of restrictive laws until the year 1900 saw restrictive laws on the books in every state in the Union.

The Legacy of Margaret Sanger

But those laws did not do away with abortion because there existed no truly effective contraceptives, nor was there any *widespread* knowledge of how to keep from getting pregnant beyond remaining celibate.

Nor did there exist any effective way to keep those so determined from the practice of abortion. One who came to believe that the answer to the problem was effective birth control (a term she herself coined) was Margaret Sanger, the founder of the organization now known as Planned Parenthood (originally called The Birth Control League of America).

Sanger's concern for women began in her own home while growing up. According to her own account, she had watched her mother wither and die, largely as the result of having had too many children too close together. Later on, as a nurse, Sanger saw more of the same: young women, old and infirm before their time because of having more children than they physically or emotionally could tolerate. All too often Sanger saw their determination to control their own fertility expressed in seeking help from back-alley abortionists or attempting to terminate pregnancies themselves.

The turning point for Margaret Sanger, and for American women, came on a steamy summer day in 1912 when she was summoned to a New York City tenement house to tend a Russian Jewish woman who was about 28 years old. The woman's husband, Jake Sachs, had come home to the cramped apartment and had found his three children crying and his wife unconscious on the floor from a self-induced abortion. Sanger did her best to patch the woman up, and after about two weeks it looked as if the patient would recover. At the end of her third week of looking in on Mrs. Sachs, the frail woman said to Sanger, "Another baby will finish me, I suppose?" Sanger gently put the woman off, but when the doctor came, discussed it with him. The doctor agreed and warned Mrs. Sachs, "Any more such capers, young woman, and there'll be no need to send for me." When Mrs. Sachs asked what she could do to prevent another pregnancy, the doctor told her, "Tell Jake to sleep on the roof."

After the doctor left, Mrs. Sachs begged Margaret Sanger, "Please tell me the secret, and I'll never breathe it to another soul." Sadly, Sanger did not know the secret. Yet. About three months after this exchange, Jake Sachs called to say his wife was sick again — with the same problem. With utter dread, Mrs. Sanger pushed herself to go to the tenement:

Mrs. Sachs was in a coma and died within ten minutes. I folded her still hands across her breast, remembering how they had pleaded with me, begging so humbly for the knowledge which was her right. I drew a sheet over her pallid face. Jake was sobbing, running his hands through his hair and pulling it out like an insane person. Over and over he wailed, "My God! My God! My God!"

After leaving the young grief-stricken husband and his three motherless children, Sanger walked through the quiet city streets for hours and finally went home. She stood in her dark apartment staring out the window, with one tragic scene after another playing itself out in her consciousness with, as she put it, "photographic clarity," for the pathetic Mrs. Sachs was only one of many:

As I stood there the darkness faded. The sun came up and threw its reflection over the house tops. It was the dawn of a new day in my life also. The doubt and the questioning, the experimenting and trying, were now to be put behind me. I knew I could not go back to merely keeping people alive.

I went to bed knowing that no matter what it might cost, I was finished with palliatives and superficial cures; I was resolved to seek out the root of evil, to do something to change the destiny of mothers whose miseries were as vast as the sky.

But how were mothers to be saved? Having been rendered sterile with the birth of her third child, she had, she said, been "spared" worrying about having too many children. Progressive women she consulted were "thoroughly discouraging." They told her, "Wait until we get the vote. Then we'll take care of that." Socialists told her, "Wait until women have more education. Wait until we secure equal distribution of wealth." Having no idea of how powerful the laws that "laid a blanket of ignorance over the medical profession" were, she asked, "Why aren't physicians doing something?" to which she was told, "The people you're worrying about wouldn't use contraception if they had it; they breed like rabbits. And besides, there's a law against it."

Not only were there specific laws banning the practice of abortion in every state, but numerous states had enacted laws that banned the practice of birth control as well. What Sanger would have to contend with in New York would ultimately be laws against pornography that made it unlawful to disseminate any

materials that made reference to pregnancy, contraception, or venereal disease. (Sanger's greatest
adversary would prove to be Anthony Comstock,
director of the Society for the Suppression of Vice in
New York City, who invoked the law against pornography to get Sanger arrested. Interestingly, Comstock,
a never-married man, like many right-to-lifers today,
was opposed to contraception as well as abortion.)

Ultimately, Sanger's fervent quest to provide women
with "the secret" led her to Europe where, shortly after
her arrival, she learned of a "German pessary"
(diaphragm), perfected by Dutch physician Dr. Aletta
Jacobs and her colleagues. Before setting off for
Holland, Sanger did some research and learned that,
apparently as a result of effective birth control, infant
and maternal mortality rates had dropped dramatically,
and that three times more mothers' lives were being
saved in that small country than in the United States.

When Sanger got to Holland and tracked down Dr.
Jacobs for the purpose of bringing the diaphragm to
American women, she was in for another surprise: in
contrast to the narrow-minded views regarding birth
control back home, Sanger found that not only did the
diaphragm come in fourteen different sizes, but it was
being sold in *shops* throughout the country!

On her return to the United States, Sanger and her
second husband, Noah Slee, founded the first doctor-
staffed birth control clinic and went on to establish
some 300 such clinics nationwide. They also persuaded
an American company to mass-produce the diaphragm.

Margaret Sanger devoted the rest of her life to the
struggle to make birth control available to all women

and often went to jail for the cause. At the time of her death in 1966, although the distribution of birth control devices was still illegal in three states, most American women had access to effective contraception, including not only the diaphragm, but spermicides, and the Pill.

An interesting footnote here is that the Pill might not have come into use had it not been for Margaret Sanger. In the early 1950's, it was Sanger who encouraged Gregory Pincus to create the first birth-control pill and raised the money for him to do it. As Dr. John Rock (who is often singly credited with the development of the Pill, but was in fact a collaborator with Pincus) has noted, there was no government or foundation support, just Margaret Sanger's influence on a woman willing to contribute the necessary funds.

For all of her efforts to end the practice of abortion once and for all, Sanger could not foresee that abortion would persist because contraception alone could never prevent the unintended pregnancies that result from carelessness, ignorance, contraceptive failure, or rape. Nor could it intervene on behalf of nature in the instance of a seriously damaged fetus. What Sanger, who wanted to prevent the practice of abortion, could not foresee is that, as long as human and natural errors occur, there will always be women driven by their own survival instincts to resort to abortion—an option, as we know, that continued to carry great risk until it became a legal one.

Chapter 3

WHEN THE LAWS CAME TUMBLING DOWN

...the Court has recognized that a right of personal privacy, or a guarantee of certain areas or zones of privacy, does exist under the Constitution.

This right of privacy, whether it be founded in the 14th Amendment's concept of personal liberty and restrictions upon state action, as we feel it is, or...in the Ninth Amendment's reservation of rights to the people, is broad enough to encompass a woman's decision whether or not to terminate her pregnancy.

Justice Harry A. Blackmun
in writing the Majority Opinion, January 22, 1973

The sudden reversal of long-standing laws and social norms touched off a fire storm among members of conservative religious groups and their political allies. Many opponents saw the decision [*Roe v. Wade*] as an assault on traditional morality and family values....Almost instantly, the right to life movement was born.

Flo Conway & Jim Siegelman
Holy Terror, 1982

The Supreme Court's 1973 ruling in the case of *Roe v. Wade* did indeed touch off a "fire storm," as Conway and Siegelman report. But the battle lines had been drawn long before, setting into motion two parallel movements that would grow and develop in response to one another, and that one day would form coalitions of many different organizations. In one corner, there would be the National Right to Life Committee, United for Life, American Life Lobby, Catholics United for Life, Catholic Right to Life, Operation Rescue, and assorted right-wing organizations such as Jerry Falwell's Moral Majority and Phyllis Schlafly's Eagle Forum. In the other, there would be the National Association for the Repeal of Abortion Laws (which would ultimately become the National Abortion Rights Action League), the National Organization for Women, Planned Parenthood, and Catholics for a Free Choice. In both camps, there would be an assortment of smaller organizations and spinoffs.

No doubt some of the seeds for both movements were sown in 1959 when the American Law Institute (ALI) developed a new penal code model. In part, this model held that abortion should be allowed under the following conditions:

1. Evidence that a pregnancy was the result of rape or incest;

2. Evidence that a fetus would develop into a seriously deformed child if brought to term;

3. Evidence that continuation of a pregnancy would result in grave impairment of a woman's mental or physical health.

It is safe to speculate that this penal code model was in response to a largely unspoken but fomenting public sentiment. By that time, we were operating under restrictive laws that supposedly had been enacted to protect women against unsafe practices. But medical technology had long since made legal abortion safer than childbirth. Thus, rather than protecting women, the laws continued to spawn avoidable tragedies.

American Tragedies Spotlighted

Although ultimately the pro-choice movement would be spearheaded by feminist and family-planning organizations, the public debate began in the early 1960's when two events made it vividly clear that contraception could never be a total answer.

The first event to push the issue of choice squarely into the consciousness of mainstream America occurred in 1962 when an Arizona television personality, Sherri Finkbine, became pregnant with her fifth child. As it turned out, this otherwise joyous event became cause for despair when it was learned that the thalidomide Mrs. Finkbine had taken to relieve her morning sickness had recently been linked to a rash of birth defects. (The drug was widely used in Europe and Mrs. Finkbine's husband, who had been abroad, had brought some home with him.)

Taken in the first trimester of pregnancy, thalidomide was found to impede the development of limbs, with the result that babies born to mothers who had taken this drug were at risk of being born with fins in place of arms, or with no legs or arms at all. On learning of its devastating side-effects, the Finkbines were in complete agreement: the pregnancy should be terminated. Arrangements were in motion at a Phoenix hospital, the board having granted its approval for a therapeutic abortion. But then, concerned that other women may have taken this drug, Finkbine contacted the medical editor of a local newspaper and gave him her story with the understanding that she would not be identified. But, because of the publicity that resulted, she was told to forget about coming into the hospital for the procedure.

Overnight, it seemed, the press had learned her identity and, as a result, there appeared newspaper accounts and editorials taking either a pro- or anti-choice position. Co-workers in offices all over the land argued with one another. Husbands, wives, and friends discussed it, sometimes straining a relationship in the positions they took. And scores of American women were forced to ponder what they might do were they in Sherri Finkbine's position.

Ultimately, Sherri Finkbine was forced to travel to Sweden to terminate her pregnancy. As things turned out, the fetus was found to be so badly deformed that its survival would have been unlikely.

The national fervor over the Finkbine case had barely died down when an epidemic of rubella (German measles) swept over the United States in 1963. An otherwise innocuous disease, it left in its wake 20,000 stillbirths and some 30,000 babies born with serious defects, including blindness, congenital heart defects, and severe mental retardation.

The epidemic raged through 1965, creating panic in pregnant women who suspected they may have been exposed to rubella. Some women quickly opted for termination of pregnancy, if they were lucky enough to have either sympathetic doctors or connections. Others were left with no choice beyond hoping that they would give birth to normal babies. Many who were without a choice became part of the statistics which can never, of course, speak to the heartbreak of giving birth to, and the difficulty in caring for, a seriously handicapped or deformed child.

There is little doubt in the minds of some observers that out of these tragedies grew considerable public support for the right to more fully choose. In fact, according to Andrew Merton "during this period, the number of prestigious groups calling for reform [of existing abortion laws] grew steadily" with the United Presbyterian Church in 1962 becoming the first major religious organization to take a stand against restrictive laws and call for reform. In 1963, the Lutheran Church and the Unitarian Universalist Association followed suit.

Three Brave, Angry Women

No history of choice would be complete without at least some mention of three brave women who, when it was an exceedingly unpopular and risky thing to do, began to organize and agitate for women to have the right to safely terminate a pregnancy.

At about the same time that public debate over abortion was just beginning to surface, Patricia Maginnis of San Francisco and Rowena Gurner of Palo Alto, California got together and formed the Society for

Humane Abortions. Out of an office in San Francisco, they held classes to explain how safe abortions were done and how women could abort themselves. In 1964, Lana Phelan of Los Angeles hooked up with Maginnis and Gurner and agreed to run a Southern California office from her home.

What drove these women to ultimately quit their jobs and devote themselves to helping other women was that each, at different times, had experienced the degradation, fear, and humiliation of being forced to seek underground abortions. Maginnis had gone to Mexico, and Gurner, via a New York referral service, had gone to Puerto Rico. Both remained outraged that they had been essentially exiled and forced to remain silent about their experiences. Lana Phelan was a young wife and mother and had been advised that another pregnancy could cost her her life, but she was not advised how to avoid it. When she became pregnant, she panicked and, because her very life depended upon it, she sought an illegal abortion.

Out of the rage and indignation of these three women, the largest underground abortion movement in the nation came into being, referring more than 5,000 women to illegal abortionists from roughly 1964 to 1973. The three of them also spent ten years, giving speeches, and writing, printing, and distributing leaflets, publishing referral lists, and risking jail to provide help to desperate women.

Maginnis and Gurner also formed the Association to Repeal Abortion Laws, which would appear to be the forerunner of the National Association to Repeal Abortion Laws (NARAL). Some insiders believe that these three women essentially started the reproductive rights revolution that ultimately swept the nation, because they cared enough about the plight of others.

The Emergence of the Right-to-Life Movement

Backing up a bit, in response to the rubella epidemic, the first bill to reform California's restrictive abortion law was introduced into the California State Legislature in 1965; it died in Committee for lack of support. But, law or no, many California doctors were openly doing procedures in cases where deformity was likely.

None of this activity was lost on the press, and when stories began appearing about these practices, Catholic obstetrician Dr. James V. McNulty of Los Angeles, a member of the state's Board of Medical Examiners, took outraged exception: "We took an oath to uphold the law. These doctors who admit doing abortions for rubella are saying they're above the law. If we don't punish them, we're guilty of malfeasance."

As a result of McNulty's efforts, many hospitals reversed their policies and put a stop to the practice. The Board of Medical Examiners charged seven physicians with performing illegal abortions on patients who had been exposed to rubella. Reaction to the crackdown, in turn, triggered organized support among the doctors for a liberalized bill, sponsored by State Senator Anthony C. Beilensen of Beverly Hills, that would ultimately be introduced into the legislature in 1967.

Meanwhile, on the east coast, in 1966, a reform bill was introduced in the New York State House of Representatives. This measure would have allowed abortion under the guidelines spelled out by the American Law Institute. Despite a groundswell of support, in part as a result of the Finkbine case and the rubella epidemic, the bill was defeated. Reintroduced in 1967, it evoked a pastoral letter from the New York Catholic bishops, sent to every diocese in the state, urging all Catholics to oppose it. The bill was again defeated.

At roughly the same time, a law was introduced in the Connecticut legislature that would have permitted abortions for rape victims and girls under the age of sixteen. Almost immediately, the three Roman Catholic bishops of Connecticut responded with a statement denouncing the proposed measure.

By this time, the tactics of the opponents of choice had moved from simple messages about protecting the unborn to accusations that anyone who disagreed was advocating genocide. John H. Terry, an Assemblyman from Syracuse, went so far as to compare the abortion of defective fetuses with the elimination of "defective Jewish persons" in Nazi Germany. Many people, however, were offended by these tactics, and on February 24, 1967, the Protestant Council of New York City, along with three Jewish organizations, issued a statement saying, "We do not feel...that the case of ecumenism is best served by attributing to us the advocacy of murder and genocide...."

The fat was in the fire. In 1967, even though virtually all attempts at reform in every state had failed, there was serious concern among anti-choice forces because the number of states in which there were campaigns to liberalize the laws had climbed from twelve to thirty-one. The Catholic hierarchy responded to this growing pro-choice tide by finally making its campaign against it official. On April 13, 1967, the National Conference of Catholic Bishops budgeted some $50,000 to begin an education campaign aimed at Catholics and non-Catholics alike, but was fast to emphasize that the church would not become involved in political action. "That," declared the Most Reverend Walter W. Curtis, of Bridgeport Connecticut, "is essentially the task of our citizens." In other words, the campaign would not be political, but the people who took their cue from the Bishops would be.

That same year in California, Catholic forces were mobilizing to defeat the new bill that Senator Beilensen had in the works, one that would permit termination of a pregnancy in the event of a possibly seriously deformed fetus. Arch-conservative James Francis Cardinal McIntyre had pulled together an organization called the Right to Life League, which featured a bureau of speakers who would, according to Andrew Merton, "go anywhere any time to deliver the anti-abortion line." Additionally, McIntyre's diocese (Los Angeles) engaged the public relations firm of Spencer-Roberts to fight to maintain the old, restrictive law. Interestingly, Merton points out, one of the other clients of the firm was Ronald Reagan, then Governor of California who, when asked by McIntyre, agreed to fight the bill, although he did eventually sign it.

When the Laws Came Tumbling Down

On April 25, 1967, just two weeks after the Catholic hierarchy in New York had begun to seriously organize, the first reform bill in the nation was signed into law in Colorado. Based on the model proposed by the American Law Institute, the measure also carried with it a requirement that three physicians review each case and confirm in writing that one of the three ALI conditions existed. The bill was not restricted to residents of Colorado, which meant that women with awareness and the means could travel to Colorado and obtain safe, legal abortions.

In May of that same year, South Carolina enacted a similar piece of legislation, but one that restricted the procedure to women who had been residents of the state for at least four years.

In California, thanks to support from the medical profession, Senator Beilensen's bill passed. But, to get the governor to sign it into law, Beilensen had to remove the one condition that was the primary reason that he and the medical profession had worked so hard: the possibility of fetal deformity as justification for termination of a pregnancy. The approved measure, as signed by the governor, would only allow termination of a pregnancy in the event of rape or incest or if continuation of pregnancy posed the threat of grave physical or mental consequences for the woman.

What this meant was that women seeking safe, legal procedures had to receive the approval of a hospital board that would certify that either they were mentally unstable or that continuation of a pregnancy would endanger their lives, or they had to *prove* they had been victims of rape or incest. What it also meant was that safe, legal abortion would be available only to those who were aware of the law, knew how to manipulate the system, and could afford a procedure performed in a hospital. What it meant in *real* terms was that the quacks were still in business in the State of California, and many women were forced to carry unintended pregnancies to term.

The following year in New York, another bill was introduced into the State Legislature and once again it was defeated. The process was repeated in 1969. That year in New York City, the National Association for the Repeal of Abortion Laws (NARAL) was officially launched after several months of organizing that had begun the summer before in Chicago. Its founders consisted of a small group of feminists, pro-choice advocates, and leaders in the population movement who were dedicated to the goal of repealing, as opposed to reforming, abortion laws across the land.

The next year, according to Merton, through a bizarre turn of events, the New York legislature voted for passage of a bill that would essentially allow abortion on request. Written by Earl Brydges, the majority leader in the New York State Senate, a man vehemently opposed to liberalization, the bill was so liberal that he thought it could never pass. But, with Brydges voting against his own bill, it passed the Senate and went on to the Assembly, where it looked as if it would go down to defeat by a majority of one. On April 9, 1970, in a twist that rocked everyone on either side of the issue back on their heels, after the roll call was completed, Assemblyman George Michaels stood up, was recognized and said, "I realize, Mr. Speaker, that I am terminating my political career, but I cannot in good conscience sit here and allow my vote to be the one that defeats this bill."

Groups that had been fighting for liberalization were jubilant. They were confident that it would only be a matter of time before other state legislatures proved to be as progressive. Indeed, between 1967 and 1970, there had been a snowballing movement toward reform at the state level. In addition to the repeal of the New York law, sixteen states had passed new liberal laws and a dozen more states had modified or partially repealed existing prohibitive laws.

And the Right-to-Life Army Came Marching In

With the liberalization of New York's law, clinics and referral services seemed to spring up overnight. And women from all over the United States traveled to what came to be called "the abortion capital of the nation."

Outside of New York, there were numerous referral services that would direct people either to New York or to other states closer to home where liberal laws had been enacted and doctors were performing abortions.

As fast as the clinics and referral services would spring up, there were picketers on hand from a fairly wide array of organizations that identified themselves as being part of the right-to-life movement. They would carry their placards proclaiming all who worked within or entered seeking services to be "baby murderers" (a tactic which later came to be known as "sidewalk counseling").

And, as fast as laws were struck down or liberalized, or looked as if they might be, the right-to-life movement would mobilize and fight to block liberalization. In June of 1970 in California, for example, the right-to-life movement turned out in full force to block passage of a bill introduced by Senator Anthony Beilensen that, in effect, was nearly identical to that which had been approved by the New York legislature.

As one who had been asked to give testimony in favor of the legislation, I had a unique opportunity to observe the emerging anti-choice movement in action before it had collectively developed the sophistication its leaders now generally display. Along with those who had come to testify on behalf of the Beilensen Bill (physicians, attorneys, and representatives from Planned Parenthood and Zero Population Growth) there was a full right-to-life contingent on hand to give counter testimony and a gallery filled with anti-choice supporters, including members from The Right to Life League, United for Life, Friends of the Fetus, The Blue Crusade Against Satan, Voices for the Unborn, and the League Against Neo-Hitlerism.

There was testimony from a woman physician who had been a pathologist at Boston General Hospital and had become sickened by performing post mortems on women and young girls who had died as a result of abortion. This was followed with testimony from a right-to-lifer who suggested that the way to deal with overpopulation was to put an atmosphere on Mars.

Shortly after another woman doctor testified to the need for access to legal abortion to serve as a back stop to contraceptive failure, another claimed that liberalized abortion laws did not serve the rights of the father of the unborn.

While right-to-life leaders gave testimony, as if on cue, their support groups in the gallery would cheer and howl. And when pro-choice advocates testified, the anti-choice contingent would hiss and throw garbage about, at one point becoming so unruly that the Chairman of the Committee threatened to clear the Senate chamber.

Then, during a break in the proceedings, when an elderly man (known to be a fixture in the capitol) strolled through the corridor carrying a sign that called for the impeachment of Governor Reagan, the right-to-life contingent turned on him, threw him to the floor, and tossed his sign away. A melee ensued, and the police had to be summoned.

In the end, after the formal hearing came to a close, the anti-choice movement gave us a hint of the power it would ultimately possess in swaying legislators. The legislation was effectively pigeonholed until such time as Senator Beilensen would take a vote on it. At this point, there seemed little likelihood of its passage. The bill was tabled, and in California, for the next three years, women seeking legal abortions had to face hospital review boards and be declared physically or mentally incompetent before being granted the procedure.

Meanwhile, in New York, the Catholic church wasted no time in issuing another pastoral letter after New York's liberalized bill was signed into law. Reaffirming its earlier position, it also warned that any Catholic who either procured an abortion or helped anyone else to do so would be immediately excommunicated from the Church. And, in 1971, opponents of the New York bill launched a drive to repeal it.

And Then It Was Over

And then, a young divorced Texas woman named Norma McCorvey became pregnant. Having had the experience of being forced to give a child up because she could not afford to raise one, she felt that there was no way that she could go through that again. She sought help from a doctor, telling him that she had been raped. There would have to be a police report, she was told. He couldn't risk it.

Enter Sarah Weddington, a young lawyer in search of a plaintiff and case to test the Texas abortion law before the United States Supreme Court. Weddington filed the case using the pseudonym of "Jane Roe" for the plaintiff to protect the identity of McCorvey. The suit was filed against Dallas County District Attorney Henry Wade for preventing Roe/McCorvey from obtaining an abortion.

On January 22, 1973, by a seven-to-two vote, the Supreme Court held in *Roe v. Wade* that the Texas law was unconstitutional: states could not restrict abortions in the first trimester of pregnancy as long as they were performed by licensed physicians; with respect to second-trimester abortions, the states could regulate conditions under which an abortion could be performed only to protect the safety of the woman; states could limit abortions performed after the point of fetal viability (in the third trimester) but could not prohibit such procedures in cases where a woman's life or health was threatened.

In another case, *Doe v. Bolton*, on that same day and also by a seven-to-two vote, the court struck down restrictions on facilities that could be used for abortions. With that decision, it became legal for abortions to be performed in clinics instead of hospitals throughout the nation.

The battle, it seemed, was over. The constant debate over women's live bodies was over. The right to choose had become the law of the land. The "victory" was so complete that one population activist, always a little annoyed at NARAL for, as he perceived it, co-opting his organization's cause, sneered, "Well, it looks like NARAL is out of business. How will it justify its existence now?"

No sooner had those words fallen from his lips than it became clear that from that moment, NARAL, more than ever, would have its work cut out for it. With repeal once and for all achieved, the next goal was to steadfastly defend it, for the right-to-life armies quickly became more galvanized into action than ever before. The anti-choice movement grew up, got rich, and developed a whole line of new and sophisticated tactics. Thus, a new NARAL was, out of necessity, born: The

National Abortion Rights Action League, whose job would prove to be ongoing and immense.

But for the moment, as never before, American women had the freedom to choose and to control their own destinies—and the legal right to save their own lives.

Chapter 4

THE WAY THINGS GOT TO BE

[I] feel abhorrence for the idea of deliberately bringing an unwanted pregnancy to term, delivering forth a helpless human being, and then just giving it away to others to care for. To never again take any responsibility whatsoever for a baby deliberately brought into this world seems to me utterly barbaric!

By contrast, abortion is absolutely moral and responsible. To stop the pregnancy and prevent the birth of a child who cannot be properly cared for shows wisdom—an understanding of the realities of life. The only life in an embryo is the woman's life within it. Until it can live a separate life, it is *not* a separate life. "Infallible" doctrines and dogmas simply wither away in the light of that fact.

Constance Robertson
in *The Religious Case for Abortion*, 1983

...a very disproportionate number of the women whose health and lives were saved by safe, legal abortion were black. (In Harlem Hospital alone, for instance in the year following the 1971 liberalization of New York State's abortion law, there were about 750 fewer admissions of women suffering from self-induced or illegal abortions.)

Gloria Steinem
in *Speak Out*, 1982

A mother I know reaches back a few years for a story that illustrates what a difference a humane court ruling can make:

It was in the spring of 1984 that I became very grateful that there were no longer laws against abortion. My daughter was going through a lot of serious emotional pain. There had been a young man that she had fallen madly in love with, and he'd treated her badly. At about the same time, she was in a car crash that traumatized her. But for the grace of seat belts, she would have been hurled through the windshield. She was left badly shaken. And as often happens in life, there was one thing after another. Her ill-fated love affair and the car crash had shaken her so much that she began to fail in school (she was in college) and was put on probation. There were big things and little things, one right after the other.

She got back together with this boyfriend very briefly, and then they broke up. On the rebound, she became involved with another young man, and one evening after a few too many glasses of wine, they went to bed.

Well, you guessed it. She became pregnant. Shaking with fear, rage, and every emotion under the sun, she told me, "I will simply kill myself."

I looked at this person—child, actually, though she was twenty-one at the time—and I realized that there was no way she could get through a pregnancy not knowing who the father was—or, even if she did, for that matter. Were she forced to do so and give up a baby for adoption, that would surely push her over the edge. I did the only sensible thing any loving mother would do. When she told me she wanted to end the pregnancy, I offered to make arrangements.

Our gynecologist, a kindly man, quickly told me that the both of us had made the right decision. Actually, he congratulated us both: "She's fortunate that she could come to you, and you're fortunate she could come to you." The procedure was without incident, and I knew when the doctor and I sat with her in recovery, the decision was the only one that could have been made. The alternative would have been to sacrifice the sanity of a twenty-one-year-old for a fetus, an embryo.

Today my daughter has her life in order. By that, I mean that she has recovered fully from what I now see was a complete emotional breakdown that would only have worsened had she been forced to continue with her very unwanted pregnancy. She has just about finished her education and looks forward to having a career and looks even more forward to the day when she will marry and have a family.

I thank God every day that I did not have to risk losing my beloved daughter to preserve the life of the fetus. Both probably would have been lost, in any case, because I know she was entertaining thoughts of suicide at the time.

Another story comes from a woman who in 1980, when she was thirty years old and had two children under the age of three, became a member of that six percent for whom birth-control pills fail. At the time, her husband was recovering from a serious illness and was unable to work full time, so she worked out of dire economic need. When her accidental pregnancy occurred, she was already pushed beyond her limits. She was rail thin and had deep circles under her eyes. Like many working mothers, her routine was grinding her into the ground: up at five in the morning, she would get herself ready for work, get her children fed and dressed, get her husband settled for the day, and off she would go, hurriedly dropping the children off at the sitter's on her way to work. After a full day, she would pick up the kids, go home, fix dinner, give the children their baths, clean house, and fall into bed, utterly exhausted, at ten or eleven.

Her husband's health had been improving steadily, and a turning point was that they were able to resume marital relations, so this woman began taking the Pill again. She was astonished when she immediately became pregnant. She was also devastated that there was only one solution to the problem: "I have only given life, never taken it. But I have no real choice," she said.

Indeed, not only was she exhausted, but often she was ill. Once, in fact, when she had bronchitis, she kept working until she collapsed because, having used up all her sick leave for family matters, she had none left to take for herself. She could not afford to take time off without pay.

She was fortunate because the local family planning clinic ran abortion clinics on Saturdays. She was able to obtain an abortion at a price she could afford and was back on the job the following Monday. "Were it not for legal abortion," she told me, "I would have stuck a coat hanger up my uterus."

About two years later, after this woman's husband had recovered enough to return to work full time, she became pregnant again. This time, it was cause to rejoice. After her baby daughter was born, she told me, "The souls have a way of getting here, you know. And this time, it really was meant to be."

Another woman recalled that a few years back, when she was thirty-eight years old and the mother of a five-year-old, she and her husband were absolutely delighted when they learned that they were to have another child. Because of her age, she underwent amniocentesis and a sonogram. The couple's delight turned to despair when it was revealed that the fetus was badly damaged and that quite likely, should she carry it to term, she would give birth to a retarded, blind baby with a vast array of organic problems. The doctor explained to them that the decision was theirs. After long and careful soul searching, the woman and her husband concluded that to bring such a child into the world would be unfair, and that the care that would be required and the open-ended problems they would face would tear their family apart. It was not an easy decision, but the only answer was abortion. Unlike others who were faced with such a situation before legalization, the woman simply told her doctor of her decision, all of the arrangements were made, and the abortion was performed without any ensuing problems. The family remains intact and, as far as this couple is concerned, was saved because they had the right to a safe, legal abortion.

An ob/gyn I spoke with said that he insisted that any of his patients who became pregnant past the age of thirty-eight or who had a family history of genetic diseases (such as muscular dystrophy, Tay-Sachs, or sickle-cell anemia, to name just a few) undergo amniocenteses to determine whether the fetus was healthy and normal. If a patient refused, his policy was to refer her to another physician. "There is far too much misery in this world," he declared, "associated with having retarded or deformed children, and that risk is great in late pregnancies. And life is difficult enough without having a child who is genetically condemned to suffer and die, those occasional happy letters about 'special children' being such a joy in Dear Abby notwithstanding."

This physician also has very strong feelings about unintended and unwanted pregnancies. Recalling his many patients of the 1950's and 1960's who got pregnant because of unreliable contraception and who became seriously depressed as a result, he said, "It's a wonderful thing to see such a difference today—to see women who really do want to have their babies. Having a choice has made that difference."

Furthermore, he said, he never hesitates to perform abortions on unmarried teenagers. They are babies themselves and have no business having babies. One case he recalled was brought to his attention by one of his patients, the mother of a teenaged daughter whose best friend thought she was pregnant. Both mother and daughter were alarmed because the pregnant friend was threatening suicide. He agreed to see the youngster and, after a pregnancy test confirmed her worst fears, he suggested that she talk it over with her own mother. She became hysterical, saying that she'd sooner die than have her mother know. At that point, he made a decision to perform an abortion—at no fee.

About two months later, he got a call from the girl's mother. The woman was outraged and threatened to sue him for performing an abortion on her minor child without her knowledge or consent. He told her to feel free to do just that. He then added, that if she were an understanding parent, her daughter would have been able to come to her; moreover, he told her, had she given her daughter adequate information and arranged for her to have birth control, this situation wouldn't have happened in the first place. And then he told me, "Lawsuit or not, I'm glad I did it, and I'd do it again. That frightened child needed help. And I'm glad the law allowed me to give it."

Even those who say that they believe that abortion is immoral under any and all circumstances may find the solution to their problems made simpler because of access to safe, legal abortion. A working mother of eight children frequently and passionately expounded on what she felt were threats to "traditional family values:"

working mothers who neglected their children, the ERA, and, of course, legal abortion. Her eyes would blaze when she said, "Abortion is murder, there are no two ways about it." Then her unmarried daughter became pregnant, and the young man who had gotten her that way was not about to become a husband and father overnight. As this distraught young woman began to make plans to have the baby and give it up for adoption, her mother intervened, thundering, "In this family, we don't give babies away." The young woman instantly took that to mean that she should have her baby and raise it in the bosom of her family. Not so! For this family did not have "illegitimate" children either, and thus Mother arranged for an abortion. The daughter complied, but felt enormous guilt for some time because the very person who had forced the abortion on her had drummed it into her head that abortion was murder.

Beyond the practical considerations involved and the fact that ideology was put to the test of reality, unmistakably, the older woman was determined to impose her will—whatever it may be at any given time—on others. Clearly, from beginning to end, she had denied her daughter the right to make her own choices.

But, the story ended happily for all concerned. The daughter came to believe that she was given a second chance, and things have turned out well for her. She is now happily married to a fine young man, and has three healthy children. With the full support of her husband who does his fair share when it comes to the children, she's now in college and doing well. As for her mother, she had opened the window wide enough to deal with the matter at hand, and then snapped it shut, her right-to-life views back firmly in place.

Another side of the coin may show itself in women who themselves have had abortions, regret having done so, and then become involved in the right-to-life movement, intent on denying to other women the right to make the same choice. One such woman is Olivia Gans of the National Right to Life Committee, who has recently become a star of sorts on national television. In one of her appearances on the Phil Donahue Show a while back, she essentially admitted that had legal abortion not been an option, she wouldn't have made a decision she later came to regret.

Both of these cases suggest that anti-choice advocates may fall into two distinct groups: those who feel compelled to run other people's lives and those who feel a deep need for something or someone to run their lives for them. This may also explain the preponderance of patriarchal males in leadership roles in the right-to-life movement and the women who, directed by the male leadership, work on behalf of having their own rights taken away. But even then, such followers sometimes make exceptions to their own rules.

"For reasons that perhaps even they don't fully understand," writes David R. Zimmerman, "many women opt for the solution they believe should be denied other women in the same situations: They have abortions." Zimmerman says that abortion providers have known for years that some of the people who seek their services are opposed to legal abortion. Such women, he says, see their own situations or the situations of their own daughters as "different" from other abortion patients, whom they see as "sluts" and "trash."

In more than one instance, health-care providers report having seen women *in picket lines protesting abortion*, only to have these anti-choice activists show up either as patients themselves or seeking abortions for their unmarried daughters.

"One of the most remarkable," one clinic director in the Midwest told Zimmerman, "was a woman who came [from another part of the state] and said she was the Right-to-Life president in her county. 'But,' she said, she 'had become pregnant and had to have an abortion'."

Another clinic director recalled having a prominent anti-choice advocate in a rural community bring his reluctant wife to a distant clinic. They had three children, he said, and they couldn't afford another.

One young woman who agreed to be interviewed told her counselor after her abortion, "I'm still against it...I have, as of right now...a very promising future, and a baby just wouldn't—couldn't have fit in for me. I don't think I could have loved it the way a child should be raised or loved. There would always be that resentment." She went on to say that she is far more liberal about abortion than many of her friends, "who oppose it even in the event of rape or if the mother's life is endangered by the pregnancy." But, she added, "I know personally that some of these same girls, the moment they found out they were pregnant, went straight to the abortion clinic...I know of some people who've actually picketed outside...and have turned around and...been in here in a few weeks to have it done."

The health-care providers interviewed all agreed that these are their most difficult patients as they see themselves as superior to the other patients, demand special treatment, and are often hostile to clinic staff members for delivering abortion services. As one such patient said as she left the operating room after her abortion, "I hope God forgives you for doing this."

One thing that is clear, according to Zimmerman, "is that these women usually leave abortion clinics with their ambivalence and conflict intact." In other words, most often, the fact that they themselves have felt compelled to obtain abortions and have been able to do so legally and safely doesn't change the way they view other women in the same situation. Nor does it alter their beliefs that abortion should be outlawed. In fact, as Janet Todd of the Cincinnati Women for Women told Zimmerman, many such women obviously believe that if the clinics didn't exist, women with such ambivalent feelings about abortion would not have to face making a decision about it.

Chapter 5

THE HIGH COST OF UNWANTEDNESS

> In the late 1970's, the age group that felt the largest percent increase in homicide was, sadly 1-4...
>
> A young, lonely, single mother may find herself chronically depressed by poverty and her inability to deal with both a job and her children. So, in her frustration, she abuses her children...
>
> Teenage mothers are more likely to abuse their children than older women. And even during the decade of the baby bust [when the birth rate dipped], the number of babies born to teenage women was increasing...some wanted babies for status, others were pathetically ill-informed about contraception...most of them tragically ill-equipped for the job [of parenthood].
>
> Landon Y. Jones
> *Great Expectations*, 1980

> The population dilemma, matched in urgency only by the possibility of nuclear war, is still the greatest threat to world peace and material improvement for most of the world's people.
>
> Stephen D. Mumford
> *The Pope and the New Apocalypse*, 1986

It does not take an accounting wizard to figure out that, in purely economic terms, there is a large price tag attached to the unintended pregnancies of those who are unable to bear the financial responsibility of having or caring for children. Focusing just on teenage, unwed mothers, Planned Parenthood estimates the dollar cost per year at $18 billion, noting that for every dollar invested in preventing teen pregnancy, more than eleven are saved. And if pregnancy cannot be prevented, obviously, the cost of terminating an unintended pregnancy, at a fee of generally around $250, costs less than a pregnancy carried to term with the cost of delivery being roughly $2,000 for a normal birth. Then, of course, there is the matter of providing for the child once it is born.

These are the cold, hard figures that should persuade virtually anyone concerned with how our tax dollars are spent that an ounce or two of prevention can save millions. But the dollar costs of unwantedness are nothing as compared to the human costs—for suffering and tragedy are not easily measured in bookkeeping terms.

A Human Tragedy

The connection between unwanted pregnancies and child abuse (including abandonment and neglect) is as old as motherhood itself. In the earliest of times, when fertility control was at best dubious, infanticide was common. In developing nations today, the practice remains more prevalent than many of us would like to believe. And, in our own well-developed United States, in the early part of this century, leaving an unwanted infant in a window or placing it outside to freeze to death was not unknown.

More disturbing, in the years since we have theoretically come a long way, it seems that every other week newspapers carry headlines which read: "Newborn Found in Shopping Bag in Park," "Woman Gives Birth on Airplane and Stuffs Infant into Garbage Receptacle," "Baby Found in Garbage Can," "Baby Thrown Out of Second Story Window: Mother Sought." It would appear that technological breakthroughs in contraception and access to abortion are not enough to eliminate abandonment altogether. When it comes to providing adequate information regarding available options, we apparently have a way to go.

Child abuse that goes beyond simple abandonment is a more complicated phenomenon. To understand how parents can be reduced to violence, consider the fact that many people who *want* the children they have find themselves on the threshold of physical and emotional child abuse. This is so even when parents are mature and have the financial resources necessary to maintain a good standard of living.

Quite coincidentally, the same year that *Roe v. Wade* gave every woman a choice in the matter, I began to take a close look at how middle-class mothers of *wanted* children felt about their roles. Very briefly, this is what I heard: "Nobody ever told me what would be involved"..."I never knew it would be twenty-four hours a day, 365 days a year"..."I feel the responsibility is overwhelming"..."I didn't know children could be so monstrous"..."I didn't know I had a temper until I had kids"..."I expected it to be wonderful from the beginning but it's been terrible"..."I never experienced such feelings of guilt and inadequacy"..."During the first six months, I forgot what it was like to get a decent night's rest"..."It was the endless crying that made me nearly flip out."

The really bad news was hearing how such frustrations caused these mothers to react: "When my baby cried and cried, I just wanted him to stop. I found myself standing over the crib with a pillow in my hand, but I caught myself just in time," said one mother. Another, in a long and agonizing letter, said, "It was at the end of a terrible day and I was cooking dinner, and I just snapped when my two-year old threw a tantrum in the middle of the kitchen floor. I grabbed him and started shaking him." "My child bit me, and I lost it," another woman said. "I was trapped in the house for weeks on end with two children who seemed to do nothing but scream, vomit, get into mischief, and make one demand after another on me. One day it all got to me," yet another mother said, "and I lashed out and just hit and hit and hit."

I even managed to hear from a few seemingly mature fathers. "I never spank," one confessed, "because if I start hitting, I just won't stop." "There is a fine line," another father said, "between discipline and child abuse. I hate to think how many times I have come close to crossing over it."

Ninety percent of all child abuse that results in serious injury is what the experts call "situational abuse." It occurs as a result of parents having unrealistic expectations of the parental role, themselves, and their children, or having endured an accumulation of stress. It is generally triggered by a crisis (sometimes even a seemingly trivial one). It happens, they say, to ordinary people who may have had their children under the best of circumstances. The abuse may be physical, emotional, or both. All of us, say the child-abuse specialists, are "potential abusers" if we have children.

Imagine then, if seemingly normal, mature parents who *wanted* their children have the potential to abuse, how much greater that potential may be for the teenager thrust into the parental role or even the mature woman who emphatically does not want to become a parent. Toss in financial problems or abject poverty, and the blueprint for child abuse is more completely drawn.

Newspaper accounts that report the incidence of child abuse represent only the tip of that blood-chilling iceberg. As Dr. Vincent Fontana, a leading expert in the field of child abuse, has said, for every one case reported, there are probably at least ten. There are, he maintains, people walking the streets who have murdered their own children, a fact they have somehow managed to conceal from the authorities. Fontana, author of the book *Somewhere a Child is Crying* (1973), calls child abuse the number one killer of children in this country. More children, he says, die at the hands of their parents or caretakers than of any other "childhood disease," including leukemia and muscular dystrophy.

But, of course, not all abused children die. Most, in fact do not, but endure childhoods filled with rituals of physical and psychological abuse, often undetected, and may grow up and take out their hostilities on society. Statistics reveal that nearly all of the inmates at San Quentin were abused as children. And many of these victims of abuse not only were unwanted, but have reported that their mothers had wanted to have them aborted. As biblical scholar Graham Spurgeon notes, "If every child is wanted and taken care of...we would virtually wipe out crime and close most of our jails..."

While not all abused children who manage to survive become hardened criminals, research shows that two-thirds can be expected to repeat the abusive patterns they have learned should they have children of their own; that is, we learn how to parent from the way we are parented and tend to treat our own children as we ourselves were treated as children. Not only does abuse generally move from one generation to the next, but as it does, it is thought to increase in severity. Thus, the cycle set in motion with mild situational abuse may, a generation or so removed, evolve into what is known as "hard core" abuse.

It is estimated that every year, some 200,000 adolescents and teenagers, mostly from middle-class families, wind up on the streets, selling their bodies to survive (Rader, 1982). In the vast majority of cases, the parents of these street youngsters don't even bother to file missing persons reports. Many of these young people were born into families where they were, at some point, wanted. Imagine these now unwanted youngsters becoming parents, either because they lack the knowledge or the means to prevent pregnancies, or because they want something of their very own to love and they deliberately have babies. Then, consider what sort of lives their children can be expected to have. And then, consider what sort of parents those children will become, assuming that they survive.

The solution is at hand. Just as Margaret Sanger made the very best effort to provide women with access to birth control to prevent abortion, our national leaders ought to make the very best effort to provide every American with factual information about the realities of parenthood, complete access to all forms of birth control, and incentives to carefully and thoughtfully plan before they become parents.

In 1973, when my concern over child abuse and neglect had reached the point where I felt compelled to put together a Parental Stress Hotline in my community, I began this task by consulting a number of people who were working closely with abusive parents and their children. At the time, I spoke with Sherrol Munce Blakely who was then the Director of the Children's Trauma Center at Children's Hospital in Oakland. She told me that the key to the prevention of child abuse was the prevention of unwanted children. Invariably, she pointed out, when people who vehemently did not want to have children were forced into doing so, the children they would have as a result were at high risk of being abused, neglected, or both.

The solution, as I said, is at hand. Technically, we have the means to make it possible for all people to make informed decisions about having children and to provide them with the means to not have children when they are ill-prepared to care for them. But, sadly, that won't happen as long as there exists the anti-choice political climate that is in evidence. In fact, when the Supreme Court ruled in the *Webster* case on July 3, 1989, paving the way for states to restrict choice for the poor (discussed in detail in Chapter 7), the court basically decreed that unwantedness is destined to be an ever-growing and devastating problem. In his syndicated column, Carl Rowan writes that, as a result of the ruling, millions of babies will be born to those "least qualified to become parents."

The cost in dollars and cents, Rowan predicts, will be astronomical, involving the need for welfare, food stamps, Medicaid, day-care centers, and "billions of dollars worth of other support, day after day." In human terms, the cost is likely to be beyond our wildest of nightmares. Besides the tragedy of poor women and girls being either forced to resort to do-it-yourself abortion or to have children they cannot care for, once again, what of the unwanted children themselves? These "court-decreed" babies will get some grudging support, says Rowan, but "they will be mostly ridiculed, scorned, abused by the very people who demand that the government tell anguished girls and women, 'Sorry, but you must deliver that baby'." There will be, Rowan warns, a multitude of children who will be hated by many and loved by so few that they can never "become more than the beasts of burden and the producers of more doomed babies."

For a frightening look into what all of this may do to our nation, we need only take a look at other nations in the world where an absence of choice has prevailed.

The Global Picture

Nowhere is it clearer that institutionalized child abuse and neglect are international phenomena than in those underdeveloped countries where famine and disease have become an almost accepted part of life, and infanticide the last desperate stab at controlling fertility. India, Bangladesh, Ethiopia, and Latin America (to a lesser, but still tragic extent) with the utter and devastating deprivation that many of their children experience come readily to mind. Yet some of us wonder at the futility of the endeavor to feed these children since those who survive will grow up and spawn still another generation so condemned. Often ignored is the reality that the last thing our beleaguered planet needs is an ongoing increase in population.

We have been fruitful and we have multiplied. And if the present trend continues, we may well multiply ourselves into oblivion. Respected authorities, such as Professor Paul R. Ehrlich of Stanford University, have warned that, without intervention, the population of most of the underdeveloped and developing nations in the world will double within the next thirty years. At the same time, the population of the developed and consuming nations (such as the United States) will continue to increase.

Long before the world's nations reach their population doubling time, warns Stephen Mumford "dire consequences would spread like an atomic cloud: Third-world families would be driven to unprecedented levels of abortion and infanticide—particularly of female babies. Developing countries would be left with massive unemployment, hideously sprawling cities, woefully inadequate food supplies, ravaged environments" and a continuing escalation of absolute poverty. Examining the living conditions of Ethiopia and Bangladesh, characterized by extreme malnutrition, illiteracy, disease, and abject misery, we can see the third world of the future in microcosm. And, perhaps in truth, we see the *whole world* of the future in microcosm as we stroll down city streets and see poverty and homelessness in our own land of plenty as we have never before seen it in our own lifetimes.

Some may argue that the problem lies in the redistribution of wealth, that when people become affluent they tend to have fewer children. It could just as easily be argued that a contributing factor to poverty, here and elsewhere, is an absence of realistic family planning, for nothing dooms a family to poverty more quickly than having more mouths to feed than they can afford.

And some may argue that the population explosion is a myth given the fact of so much remaining open space the world over. But, as Robert Ornstein and Paul Ehrlich point out, crowding "is the *least* significant aspect of overpopulation." As a matter of fact, they say, "The entire human population of earth could stand on one thousand square miles." But what is significant is that between 1923 and 1982, "the world population more than doubled, and during that same period, the environment deteriorated more than at any other time...." Furthermore, they say that the long-term carrying capacity of the earth has already been exceeded "because we are rapidly destroying the resources needed to support 5 billion people."

When enough of our natural resources are gone, say Ornstein and Ehrlich, "the population seems doomed to drop below current levels." This is a very gentle, understated way of telling us that if we do not control population growth, then pollution, famines, and other negative effects of overpopulation will do it for us.

China, having seen the writing on the wall, has adopted policies and programs designed to prevent such a disaster. When its population reached the breaking point, the government felt compelled to impose restrictions on the number of children any family could have.

The result, in contrast to other developing nations in which the average woman gives birth to five children, is that the average Chinese woman gives birth to two. And despite the availability and widespread use of contraceptives, *China is still heavily dependent on abortion to curb its population growth.*

As Mumford observes, "Though contraception as a means of limiting family size and population growth is doubtless preferable to abortion, voluntary abortion is still necessary in many developing countries as a fertility control measure, and will continue to be for some time."

Chapter 6

RU 486 TO THE RESCUE: CAN TECHNOLOGY SAVE US?

In a sense, the reality of abortion signals social failure; it is the failure of millions of individuals to *prevent* pregnancy through using contraceptives and the failure of governments in the developing world to fill the unmet need for family planning. It is the failure of birth control technology in its touted role as a perfect foil to unwanted pregnancy. And it is the failure of societies that place a higher value on the number of children a woman has than on the life of the woman herself.

Jodi L. Jacobson
World Watch, March-April 1988

The ongoing conflict between those who believe a woman has a right to end an unwanted pregnancy and those who would deny that right under any circumstances has become loud enough to create a din. But the victory scored by the right-to-life movement, a fanatic minority group, against a drug that could make abortion safer, easier, and cheaper in the United states has been a quiet and insidious one.

Maureen Dezell
The Boston Globe, March 17, 1989

Even if *Roe v. Wade* stands, the pro-choice forces had better gear up for another fight: the battle over RU 486, the controversial and often misunderstood "abortion pill."

Newsweek, April 17, 1989

Two decades ago, I recall Dr. Paul Ehrlich warning that it was folly to think that overpopulation is not a serious threat because "technology will save us" from such problems as global starvation and environmental deterioration. One needs only to look at those problems, which have steadily worsened in the twenty years since Ehrlich issued his warning, to see the truth of his words: more people than ever are starving, pollution of our air and water has never been so bad, and more natural resources are in danger of running out.

While the promise that "technology will save us" has certainly proven to be a hollow one, it could, in fact, be kept. Not by miracles in agriculture and patchwork environmental programs, but by making it possible for women the world over to safely and easily limit the size of their families.

The Failure of Family Planning

Beyond religion and politics—distinct barriers to global family planning, to be sure—there exist some basic problems in classical approaches. For one thing, many people do not fully grasp how reproduction occurs, as evidenced by explanations given even in developed nations for unintended pregnancies. "I didn't think you could get pregnant the first time," is not an uncommon explanation heard in American clinics. Then there's the dismayed teenager who complains that birth control didn't work: "I took one of my mother's birth-control pills just before." One American midwife said that when she asked her patients how they got pregnant, in an effort to determine whether contraceptive failure had taken place or whether they were using contraceptives correctly, she was stunned to learn that a number of them really didn't know where babies come from. "It hit me in a wave," she told me, "that many did not make the connection between sexual activity and pregnancy."

If some literate teenagers in a literate culture do not understand that swiping one of Mom's birth control pills won't prevent pregnancy, believe an assortment of myths, or don't know where babies come from, how can we expect to properly educate the multitudes in the rest of the world?

International family planners have their work cut out for them. In developing nations, assuming the political climate allows for birth-control education, the process begins with gaining the confidence of the people in rural communities by first providing a range of other health care and services. According to Population Communications International (PCI), this earns the health worker "the respect of the villagers. At that point, family planning is more readily accepted." The next step is reproductive education and providing birth control along with careful instruction to insure its correct use. Just to get to this point, takes not only a lot of money, but a lot of time. And with the population bomb ticking away, time is running out.

Furthermore, reproductive education and teaching people to use contraceptives properly can be tricky. A classic example of the failure of reproductive education is a story of what happened in India a couple of decades ago when citizens were shown how to use condoms. To discreetly demonstrate the process, instructors unrolled condoms onto the handles of brooms. When, several months later, there was no appreciable decrease in the number of unintended pregnancies, it was learned that some of the subjects had faithfully adhered to the instruction, carefully putting condoms on broom handles before they had sexual intercourse.

Whether or not people make all of the necessary connections between sex and reproduction and practice contraception, women the world over have a strong desire to control their own fertility. The Population Institute informs us that, worldwide, the average woman has two *unplanned* pregnancies during her lifetime. Underscoring the difficulties that international family planners face, according to Jodi L. Jacobson, most unplanned pregnancies occur because of poor access to, and inconsistent use of, contraceptives: "Poor supply and distribution networks are part of the problem, compounded by the fact that few of the birth control methods currently available fit the lifestyles or pocketbooks of potential users. Moreover, only a handful of countries have put family planning and reproductive health care at the top of their agendas."

One result of the failure of family planning is an increase in population growth, obviously. Another, that attests to the determination of women to control their fertility is that, of the 50 million abortions performed worldwide every year, roughly 20 million are *illegal*. And the tragedy is that, in cultures where women are forced to seek illegal procedures, 150,000 to 200,000 women die each year from botched abortions.

The greater tragedy is that the technology exists that could at once wipe out this human suffering and significantly curb population growth, but it is presently being kept from the world.

A Scenario

A French pharmaceutical house perfects a drug that holds an important key to wiping out much of what ails the ecological and social order of the world.

Because this relatively easy-to-administer drug can safely terminate an early unintended pregnancy, for the first time, there is genuine hope that population growth can be curbed. And there is hope that child abuse, now epidemic, can be reduced by insuring that most of the world's children will be wanted. Last, but not least, the trauma of surgical abortion can be avoided for most of the world's women and girls. On top of all of these known potential benefits to humankind, the drug is being studied for the treatment of glaucoma (which can cause blindness), endometriosis (which often causes infertility in women), Cushing's Syndrome (a disease of hormone imbalance), and that killer of millions of women, breast cancer.

But, because of the pressures brought to bear by an American-based coalition of religious organizations, the French company decides not to produce or distribute the drug. Fortunately, for the people of France, the government intervenes and orders the company to make the drug available.

Unfortunately, for the rest of the world (with the exception of China), because of continuing pressure from the religious coalition, the company decides not to license pharmaceutical houses in other countries to manufacture and test the drug. Meanwhile, back in the United States, just for good measure, the religious groups busily lobby the Food and Drug Administration to deny approval, and they threaten American companies that have shown interest in the drug with boycotts of their other products.

This scenario may sound like science fiction, but it's not! This is the way things are *now* concerning the drug RU 486. Popularly referred to as "the month-after pill," RU 486 could possibly change the fate of the world. It could reduce global population growth and its companions, poverty and pollution, and alleviate the suffering of women and their families the world over.

The drug was developed by a French scientist, Prof. Etienne-Emile Baulieu. Administered during the first trimester of pregnancy, RU 486 imitates a natural process that occurs in more than half of all pregnancies: it causes a spontaneous abortion that, like a natural miscarriage, is essentially like a heavy menstrual period.

According to a report in *Newsweek*, RU 486 works by blocking the action of the hormone progesterone, without which the lining of the uterus breaks down and is expelled with the fertilized egg. Two days after this occurs, an injection of prostaglandin is given that causes uterine contractions and ensures that the abortion is complete. RU 486 has been approved for use only in the first five weeks after conception, when it is safe and effective 95 percent of the time. There is some inconvenience and discomfort, of course, but RU 486 is safer than surgical abortion for the obvious reason that it avoids the hazards of anesthesia and the risk of perforating the uterus; and, it is certainly safer than the *illegal* abortions that are practiced by millions of women the world over.

Roussel-Uclaf, the developer of this drug, withdrew the pill only one month after its introduction, according to *Newsweek*, "as a result of extreme pressure brought by the United States' right-to-life militants...There were demonstrations in France, thousands of angry letters, some threatening unspecified violent action."

Two days after RU withdrew the drug, the French government ordered the company to resume sales. RU complied , "but its parent company, Hoescht AG, based in Germany, announced that the drug would not be distributed outside France and China (where it has also been approved) for an indeterminate period."

"We didn't threaten Hoescht-Roussel with a boycott," said Richard Glasow, a spokesperson for National Right-to-Life. "We just said that was a possibility." According to Glasow, an international anti-choice group to which the Right-to-Life belongs has instituted a boycott in Europe against products made by affiliates of Roussel-Uclaf. "We asked them to not bring the abortion pill to the U.S.," said Glasow. "We pointed out to them that we have encouraged members to boycott" another company that makes drugs used in clinical abortions. Dr. Jack Willke, President of the National Right to Life Committee, has met with other national anti-choice groups to plan a boycott of all products made by Hoescht as well as French goods: "If French winegrowers are worried, they will go to the minister of health and tell him where to go."

One consequence of the right-to-life movement's interference in the licensing of the drug will be the development of an international black market. Women desperate enough to risk their lives at the hands of butchers will not hesitate to take a black-market pill. A sense of caution is not something that characterizes desperation. With the understanding of human nature that history provides, the wise course would be to do everything in our power to insure the safe administration of this drug in a clinical setting instead of allowing it to become the pharmaceutical equivalent of the back-alley abortionist.

A point to remember is that during this entire period that the war against RU 486 has gone on, the right to terminate a pregnancy in the United States has remained a legal one. In this light, it is rather amazing that the American right-to-life movement, a minority group, has had the power to keep this drug that could alleviate the need for surgical abortion in 75 percent of all cases out of the reach of American women. It is even more amazing that this American-based movement has had the power to deny access to this drug to most of the rest of the world, when the fate of the world itself may be at stake.

Chapter 7

THE FUTURE OF CHOICE

> I am often asked, "Aren't you happy now that the struggle is over?" But I cannot agree that it is. Though many disputed barricades may have been leaped, you can never sit back, smugly content, believing that victory is forever yours; there is always the threat of it being snatched from you. All freedom must be safeguarded and held...
>
> Margaret Sanger, 1938

> I fear for the future. I fear for the liberty and equality of the millions of women who have lived and come of age in the 16 years since *Roe* was decided. I fear for the integrity of, and public esteem for, this Court.
> For today, at least, the law of abortion stands undisturbed. For today, the women of this Nation still retain the liberty to control their destinies. But the signs are evident and very ominous, and a chill wind blows.
>
> Justice Harry A. Blackmun
> Dissenting in the matter of
> *Webster v. Reproductive Health Services*, July 3, 1989

The Power, the Glory, and the Conservative New Right

"What do I care if the Pope is against birth control," one politically apathetic woman remarked. "I'm not Catholic." Well, the fact of the matter is, how the

Pope feels about birth control can directly affect whether an atheist or a Buddhist is able to practice it, if what the Pope desires becomes the law of the land.

Recall that in 1967 the "non-political" Catholic Church adopted a pastoral letter taking a position against abortion, but stopped short of putting its fingers directly in the political pie, charging the most faithful of the laity with carrying out the anti-choice mission more-or-less independently. In 1975, no doubt in response to *Roe v. Wade*, the hierarchy became more blatantly political and formulated a "Pastoral Plan for Pro-Life Activities," which stipulated that the Church itself would become more openly involved in electoral politics at all levels: local, state, and federal. Pulling out all the stops, the Church would work to elect officials who would adhere to Vatican-ordained positions and would organize congressional districts in every state. The Pastoral Letter also emphasized that passage of a "Human Life Amendment" to the United States Constitution was essential to the cause of making abortion in the United States illegal.

Among other things, this new Pastoral Plan very specifically stated that an effort should be made to demonstrate to the public that rather than right-to-life being a Catholic movement, it was non-sectarian. That same year, the Mormon church came out strongly against abortion. According to Connie Paige, Church patriarch Ezra Taft Benson proclaimed that abortion "jeopardized future membership in the Kingdom of God."

Moving right along and into Campaign '78, the Catholic Right-to-Life Committee scored some victories, namely the election of ultraconservative anti-choice Senators Roger Jepsen of Iowa, Jesse Helms of North Carolina, Rudy Boschwitz of Minnesota, and Republican Congressman Larry Pressler of South Dakota.

Meanwhile, the fundamentalist Protestant movement, under the leadership of televangelists Jerry Falwell, Tim LaHaye, Pat Robertson, and others, was growing at an unprecedented rate—and was becoming more politicized than ever before. In the past, fundamentalists generally did not vote because involvement in political activity was perceived as "worldly." As Connie Paige explains this turn of events, at the instigation of their preachers, fundamentalist Christians were suddenly becoming interested in politics. Moreover, fundamentalism was catching the attention of "right-wing ideologues, some of whom were bankrolling their own personalized preachers and using the occasion of the religious awakening to try to institute their own brand of politics," namely that of turning the United States into a Christian nation.

And then, in January of 1979, according to Paige, abortion was introduced to the fundamentalist movement, which heretofore had not concerned itself with that particular issue. As Paige tells it, this occurred when a meeting of high-ranking political conservatives who were also right-to-lifers met with Jerry Falwell and persuaded him that abortion was a politically viable issue and one he should place high on his agenda.

Falwell was so persuaded, and he made abortion a central issue of his Moral Majority.

By 1980, whether by design or accident, one goal of the Pastoral Plan was achieved. There appeared on the scene a broad-based, strongly anti-choice coalition that demonstrated its political clout by claiming responsibility for the defeat of three pro-choice or liberal veterans in the United States: Frank Church (who had never declared himself as pro-choice, but who was liberal), George McGovern, and Birch Bayh. McGovern expressed utter dismay that he was labeled a "baby murderer" because he supported choice. In speaking before a group of educators in 1982 at the University of Indiana, Birch Bayh expressed similar dismay and provided his audience with more detail.

A "born-again Christian" himself, Bayh explained that on the Sunday before his last bid for re-election, some 8,000 evangelical recruits to the right-to-life movement spent their morning putting leaflets on cars in church parking lots proclaiming Birch Bayh to be a "baby murderer." Spurred on by this churchly campaign, the faithful (many of whom, as noted, had not been voters in the past) turned out in record numbers to vote the way their ministers told them to. And Indiana rejected a man it had sent to the U.S. Senate for four terms.

With the fundamentalists, Mormons, and Catholics all committed to the issue, the right-to-life movement had become quite ecumenical. No longer could it be

84 *Over Our Live Bodies*

viewed as Catholic, which must have delighted the Bishops. But, as both Connie Paige and Andrew Merton remind us, the right-to-life movement initially was the creation of the Roman Catholic Church. The church provided the organizational structure, the money, and a nationwide network easily converted into a political machine. However diverse the movement came to appear with respect to its religious underpinnings, without the Catholic Church, it would not exist today.

The Erosion of Choice Since *Roe v. Wade*

At least once every year, Gallup, Harris, CBS, *The New York Times*, *The Los Angeles Times*, or *USA Today*, or some other monitor of public opinion publishes the results of a poll on how Americans feel about legal abortion. And, over and over again, somewhere between two-thirds and three-fourths of those polled say they favor it. Even a majority of those who say they do not generally approve of abortion are opposed to legislation that would make abortion illegal (and this, by the way, includes members of the Catholic laity).

And yet, despite this overwhelming public support for choice, during the years since *Roe v. Wade*, there have been numerous efforts to erode the intent of that decision:

- The increasing number of states that have limited minors' access to abortion by requiring either parental or judicial consent for the procedure.

- The repeated refusal of the U.S. Congress to permit Medicaid funding for abortions for poor women even in the event of rape and incest.

- An Indiana juvenile court judge's injunction in response to a suit brought by a man claiming to be the father, preventing an 18-year-old unmarried woman from obtaining an abortion.

- Utah's enforcement of a spousal notification law. In one case, an 18-year old woman's husband was notified of her visit to a clinic, whereupon he was granted a temporary restraining order to prohibit her from obtaining an abortion and from leaving the state. He also filed for divorce and for the custody of the couple's already living child and the embryo the woman was carrying.

- A case filed in Pennsylvania, designed to restrict a minor's rights to privacy, which requires poor women to report incidents of rape and incest before receiving Medicaid funds for abortion.

- The California Legislature's repeated passage of a right-to-life backed measure that would deny state funding of abortions for the state's poor women.

For the tenth consecutive year, the funding was restored by the California Supreme Court which ruled that the measure was unconstitutional.

- Michigan's 1988 referendum that would ban publicly financed abortions except to save the life of the mother.

- Colorado's failed effort to reverse a 1984 ban on financing abortions. (The 1988 effort failed by a 60-40 vote.)

- Arkansas voters' 1988 approval of an "Unborn Child Amendment" to the State Constitution by a vote of 52 to 48 percent. The amendment defines life as beginning at conception and forbids the use of state funds for abortion.

- The call of 19 states for a Constitutional Convention to outlaw abortion.

- The United States Supreme Court's agreement in January 1989 to hear the Missouri case of *Webster v. Reproductive Health Services*. According to a bulletin issued by the National Organization for Women, "The Reagan/Bush Justice Department handpicked this case as the best vehicle for overturning *Roe v. Wade*."

On July 3, 1989, in a five-to-four ruling, the Supreme Court upheld the Missouri law which holds that life begins at conception, and restricts the use of public money, medical personnel, or facilities in performing abortions. While this was thought to be devastating to choice, the Court did not overturn *Roe*, as the administration and the right-to-life movement had hoped for. Nor was this particular ruling expected to have an immediate impact on the legality of abortion nationwide. For instance, in both California and New York, abortion remained legal as of the moment. Some question remained, after the ruling, whether abortion would be outlawed in those states that had specific restrictions on the books; for example, some observers believed that states to watch would be Arkansas, Idaho, South Dakota, Louisiana, Mississippi, and, of course, Missouri because all had restrictive laws in place at the time of the ruling.

Rather than the effects being immediate, the *Webster* ruling paves the way for every state in the union to pass restrictive laws in accordance with the specific points set down by the court. As spelled out by the *New York Times* on July 4, 1989:

- Public hospitals or other taxpayer-supported facilities may not be used for performing abortions not necessary to save life, even if no public funds are expended.

- Public employees, including doctors, nurses and other health care providers, may not perform or assist an abortion not necessary to save a woman's life.

- Medical tests must be performed on any fetus thought to be at least 20 weeks old to determine its viability.

In states that adopt legislation similar to the Missouri measure, the net effect is that poor women will not have access to safe abortions.

Even though *Roe* was not overturned, there are indications that it will be. As Justice Blackmun noted in his dissent, in ruling in favor of *Reproductive Health Services*, the Court essentially invited states to pass additional laws that would more specifically test *Roe*. And, in fact, the Court has agreed to hear arguments for three such cases. Most telling is that immediately after the *Webster* ruling was made public, Jack C. Willke, President of the National Right to Life Committee, hailed it as "a major victory."

Now then, this "victory" did not happen overnight. It was the result of years of careful planning and largely the end result of three major forces:

1. A strong, well-financed, and church-backed effort able to clog the courts with test cases to take to the Supreme Court and to lobby for the passage of

state legislation that would be in place and be enforceable if *Roe* is overturned.

2. A complacent pro-choice majority that came to take the right to choose so for granted as to believe that it could never be taken away.

3. The election of a president in 1980, in some measure because of that complacent pro-choice majority, who would be sympathetic to the anti-choice position. Not only did many people take choice for granted and doubt that Reagan could take it away, they simply did not place the issue high on their priority lists.

Put simply, the July 3 ruling illustrates the power of a president to circumvent the will of the people by stacking the Supreme Court with justices likely to vote anti-choice when a test case presented itself.

It took eight years, but Reagan kept his promise to conservatives that he would do what he could to outlaw abortion. For *more* than eight years, the activists in the pro-choice movement warned of this possibility. And they warned, and continue to warn, that the makeup of the Supreme Court will not change in the foreseeable future: Sandra Day O'Connor, Antonin Scalia, and Anthony Kennedy, who made this decision possible, are all young and are on the bench for life. The only change likely with a conservative president in office is that, as older justices retire, nominees to replace them will veer further to the right. While an aroused public can block confirmation of such nominees by letting their senators know of their disapproval, we have now seen the difficulty in this. Because of the public outcry against conservative nominee Robert Bork, the Senate did not confirm his nomination. However, it became clear that any Reagan nominee would be conservative, so ultimately, the public grew weary and conservative AnthonyKennedy was confirmed. The lesson learned in not voting choice should be self-evident.

In any case, buoyed by this "victory" that Willke speaks of, the right-to life movement is prepared to go the distance. Immediately after the high court ruled on July 3, 1989, its leaders vowed that they would not stop until abortion was completely illegal in America. To this end, they declared that they would work for the passage of laws that would outlaw abortion in every state, bring additional test cases forward to overturn *Roe*, and work for the passage of a "Human Life Amendment" to the Constitution of the United States.

A Human Life Amendment

Of all of the various ways the anti-choice movement is working to turn back the clock, the realization of the ultimate goal of a "Human Life Amendment" to the Constitution of the United States would be the most far-reaching. In every one of its incarnations it has held that life begins from the very instant of conception.

Thus, enactment of such a measure could possibly mean:

- Abortion, under any and all circumstances would be considered murder. Even to preserve the life of a mother or in the case of rape or incest, abortion would be against the law of the land.

- Use of IUD's or any drugs that prevent implantation of a fertilized egg would be against the law.

- Even in the case of an ectopic pregnancy (pregnancy in the fallopian tubes which cannot result in a live birth and which is extremely dangerous to a woman), abortion would be against the law.

- Any pregnant woman who does not properly care for herself to insure the health and well-being of the fetus could be charged with child neglect. (Even without the Amendment, one California woman has been so charged.)

- Miscarriages could be subject to legal scrutiny to ascertain that a woman who miscarried did nothing to bring about the termination of a pregnancy.

As for what the future may hold, that pretty well depends on how successful the anti-choice movement is in achieving its various stated goals. Their success, it should be emphasized, depends on how much resistance they get from the pro-choice majority. Although the outcome of the struggle cannot be predicted, one prediction that can be safely made is that a future without choice would be essentially a replay of the past.

One single mother of three offered this perspective: "You know, when push comes to shove, which women will lose their rights first. First, it will be women of color, especially if they happen to be poor, as most of us sadly are. We are the last hired, the first fired, and the first to be disenfranchised by the system. It's always been that way." And then she looked at me long and hard and said, "And next will come poor white women. And after that, all women who aren't rich. And even a few who are, if they don't know their way around."

It doesn't have to be this way. Read on.

Chapter 8

PRESERVING CHOICE: AN ACTIVIST'S GUIDE

> I think the Supreme Court's decision in *Roe v. Wade* was wrong and should be overturned. I think America needs a human life amendment...I promise the President hears you now and stands with you in a cause that must be won.
>
> President George Bush
> Speaking to Anti-Choice Demonstrators
> January 23, 1989

> I'm sick of hearing people conjure up gibberish about nature as if "she" were some benevolent deity from Oz. Spring is natural. So are earthquakes and tetanus. Birth is natural, it can also be cruel. Death is natural, and it can be kind. In any case, there is no "law of nature" proscribing abortion. What we have to be worried about are the laws of men.
>
> Robert Liner, M.D.
> Letters-to-the-Editor
> *San Francisco Chronicle*, February 3, 1989

The "Right-to-Lie" Movement

So named by the California Committee to Defend Reproductive Rights (CDRR), the right-to-life movement has certainly earned this edited label.

To prove it, CDRR filed a lawsuit in March of 1986 against A Free Pregnancy Center (AFPC), asking the court to force AFPC to stop advertising itself as a clinic, birth-control center, or family planning agency on the grounds that AFPC provided only anti-abortion information and propaganda. CDRR also asked the court to stop AFPC from disseminating false and misleading information on the dangers of abortion and to stop sending fraudulent letters and making fraudulent statements to teenagers and their parents in order to intimidate women into carrying pregnancies to term.

Like some 2,000 centers scattered across the nation, AFPC had been masquerading as an abortion clinic, reaching out to pregnant women, generally the poor, the young, and the frightened. The practice of these agencies is to offer a free pregnancy test, and while the woman awaits the results, she is bombarded with visuals of aborted fetuses. Often in centers that operate under such banners as "Problem Pregnancy Counseling Service" and "Crisis Pregnancy Center," she is treated to a film or two.

One of the movies shown to the unsuspecting is what Diana Workman calls the "science-fiction film," *The Silent Scream*: "This shows an ultrasonographic depiction of a fetus in utero, the uterus itself, the abortion instruments, the 'abortionist'." It does not, Workman points out, show the woman, for that would draw attention away from the fetus. At one point in the film, the fetus appears to open its mouth as if it is screaming, though there is no scientific evidence to support that this is what actually happens. Another film, presumably designed to depict abortion as a harrowing experience, *does* feature the woman as the star: in this film, she is supposed to be screaming; the miracle here is that she's also supposed to be unconscious.

The result of such screenings, predictably, is that the frightened pregnant woman becomes too traumatized to go through with an abortion. What happens after that, in many cases, is anybody's guess. Perhaps she has the baby and gives it up for adoption; perhaps she has the baby and winds up living on the street; perhaps she has the baby and tosses it into a garbage can.

In any event, in addition to its suit against AFPC, CDRR also filed a suit against the Pearson Foundation, which distributes a manual on starting your own "Pro-Life Outreach Pregnancy Center." The manual offers advice on every facet of organizing and specifically advises would-be organizers to "try to find a building like a medical office, as opposed to a building with a homey atmosphere. You want your office to look like an abortion clinic."

In February of 1988, the court ruled in favor of CDRR. The message, clearly, was that these outfits *deliberately* sought to deceive women seeking abortions.

In any contest, the first step toward victory is understanding the opposition. Something important to keep in mind is that right-to-lifers will stop at nothing to realize the goal of denying choice to women. If lying, distorting the truth, or misleading the general public serves that end, such are justified, they feel. The goal, they say, is to save the lives of unborn children. But, as Marjory Skowronski so eloquently put it, "There is a difference between holding an opinion about abortion based on personal belief, and presenting information on abortion which is simply untrue. If a person's or agency's position is based on dishonest information, it is easy to doubt the motivation involved." If the motivation is not as stated, what then might it be?

While it is undoubtedly true that there are individual right-to-lifers whose primary concern is the life of the unborn, there appear to be a number of contradictions where the movement in general is concerned. It seems that the passionate concern for the unborn dissolves once they are born. Just for openers, the hundreds of thousands of dollars it must take to finance a large lobbying organization, travel expenses, fines, and legal fees for demonstrators who appear *en masse* at birth control clinics could feed many hungry mouths. At the same time, where are the angry demonstrators when it comes to protesting state and federal cutbacks in prenatal and postnatal care for the poor?

Closer to the truth, some observers believe, is the matter of control. Where the Catholic hierarchy, specifically, is concerned, Connie Paige points out that the church has, in fact, lost control over its membership. Increasingly, members of the flock, in open defiance of the church, she says, are involved in living-together arrangements, practicing birth control, and seeking abortions. In fact, according to *RCAR Options*, of those women who report belonging to a denomination, "The abortion rate for Catholic women is 30 percent higher than that of Protestant women...Catholic women are more likely than those of other denominations to choose abortion for fear of others discovering their pregnancy." Rather than the issue being concern for the unborn, it is more likely that the best way to make Catholic women obey the law of the Church is to make them obey the law of the land. To a slightly lesser degree, the same may hold true for the evangelicals and the Mormons.

Setting the Record Straight

While deceiving scared, pregnant girls and misrepresenting the motives behind the movement may be serious deceptions, they represent just two of the untruths put out by the anti-choice movement. The following is a collection of some of the more common right-to-life stretchings of the truth and some honest answers to help you set people straight.

Fiction: The United Supreme Court ruling in the case of *Roe v. Wade* allowed abortion on demand right up until the ninth month of pregnancy.

Fact: *Roe v. Wade* held that states could not restrict abortions in the first trimester of pregnancy as long as they were performed by licensed physicians; during the second trimester, the states could regulate conditions under which an abortion could be performed only to protect the safety of the woman; states could limit abortions performed in the third trimester, but could not prohibit such procedures in cases where a woman's life or health was threatened. Significantly, 91 percent of all abortions are performed during the first trimester, and less than 1 percent are performed during the third trimester.

Fiction: The majority of Americans disapprove of abortion and would like to see it outlawed.

Fact: While it is true that many Americans disapprove of abortion, according to a Gallup poll conducted on January 22, 1989, 75 percent of those polled do not wish to see abortion outlawed.

Fiction: Family planning clinics coerce women to choose abortion.

Fact: Not only do family planning clinics require counseling and suggest alternatives to abortion, but some provide a range of services, including prenatal care and birthing. If a woman expresses doubts, she is usually discouraged from going through with an abortion and, in some cases, turned away.

Fiction: Pro-choice advocates coerce minority women, especially the poor, into having abortions, because their ultimate goal is to reduce their populations.

Fact: The majority of those who seek abortions are white, middle-class American women. Furthermore, it has been shown that the decline in the death rate and the incidence of infertility as a result of botched abortion was more pronounced among poor minority women, after legalization, than in any other group.

Fiction: Women who have abortions suffer more psychological disturbance than those who carry pregnancies to term and give their children up for adoption.

Fact: C. Everett Koop, former Surgeon General of the United States and a staunch opponent of abortion, after examining over 200 studies, found no scientifically valid evidence to support that claim.

Fiction: Abortion is exploitive of women.

Fact: Abortion is a *choice* some women make, and
           having a *choice* removes exploitation from the
           equation. Recall that history has shown that
           while, ostensibly, restrictive abortion laws
           were enacted to protect women from unsafe
           procedures, there is reason to believe that
           such laws were at least partially enacted to
           keep midwives and other "irregulars" from
           cutting into the "business" of physicians.
           Furthermore, there is nothing that exploits a
           woman as much as forced pregnancy.

Fiction: The Bible says that abortion is immoral.

Fact: Abortion is not discussed in the Bible.

Fiction: Pro-choice advocates are "pro-abortion."

Fact: *Nobody* is "pro-abortion." In fact, the choice
           issue is not about abortion. It is about *who
           decides* whether or not a woman can choose
           that particular alternative: the woman or the
           state. Furthermore, many pro-choice advo-
           cates are personally opposed to abortion and
           would not choose it for themselves, but feel
           that their personal views should never be
           legislatively imposed on others. And some
           pro-choice advocates worry that if the state
           can decide the matter, such may open the
           door to forcing women to have abortions, in

the event, for example, that overpopulation poses a serious threat.

Fiction: Most right-to-lifers would make an exception in the case of rape or incest or to save the life of the mother.

Fact: Take a look at the record: as a result of pressure brought to bear on our national legislators, Medicaid funding has already been restricted for victims of rape or incest; prominent right-to-lifers such as Nellie Gray (March for Life) flat-out say that there should be no exceptions—that abortion should never be allowed under any circumstances; and when private citizen Larry Klein sought to have an abortion performed on his comatose wife because he was advised that her chances of survival would be improved, right-to-lifers instantly made efforts to block the abortion. More importantly, never forget that with a Human Life Amendment in place, Mr. Klein may have wound up without a legal leg to stand on. Whether or not it is a good and just one, the law is the law. The issue was who gets to choose.

Membership has its Privileges...and Power

The best defense against the dishonest tactics of the anti-choice movement is to be completely informed at all times. And one of the privileges of membership in a pro-choice organization is receiving regular mailings that report what is going on. The following national organizations approach choice from different angles:

The National Abortion Rights Action League (NARAL) is a political-action lobbying organization that is focused on one issue only. It has long been geared to blocking passage of anti-choice legislation through public education and political activity. To join and receive the newsletter and periodic Action Alerts, send $20.00 to:

National Abortion Rights Action League
1011 Fourteenth Street, N.W., 5th Floor
Washington, DC 20005

Voters for Choice is an independent, nonpartisan, political action committee (PAC) dealing with this issue. The organization raises funds for, and contributes to the campaigns of both Republican and Democratic pro-choice candidates. In the past, Voters for Choice has focused on national candidates, but it is now preparing to work in individual state campaigns. They publish a strategy guide that tells you how to answer questions posed by right-to-lifers and gives technical information to individuals who want to get involved on a local level. Contributions are welcomed, but unnecessary. You can obtain the strategy guide by writing to:

Voters for Choice
2000 P Street, N.W., #307
Washington, DC 20037

Planned Parenthood works to preserve reproductive freedom of choice and deliver services at several levels: public education, a network of clinics that provide all birth-control services, some lobbying, and working through the courts. You will be put on their mailing list if you send even $5.00 to:

Planned Parenthood Federation of America
810 Seventh Avenue
New York, NY 10019.

The National Organization for Women (NOW), a political-action and lobbying organization, has a broader agenda which includes, among other things, passage of the Equal Rights Amendment, comparable pay, public-supported day-care, and freedom of choice. NOW is currently engaged in a full-scale effort to make RU 486 available to the women of America. The newsletter, *NOW Times* is worth the price of the $25.00 membership. The address is:

The National Organization for Women
P.O. Box 7813
Washington, DC 20044

The RU 486 Task Force is committed to making RU
486 available. A single-issue organization, it focuses on
educating the general public and creating a groundswell
of support for RU 486. To obtain an informational
packet of materials, a button and a bumper sticker that
proclaims, "RU 486 to the Rescue," send $10.00 to:

RU 486 Task Force
1348 Commerce Lane, Suite 244
Santa Cruz, CA 95060

Men Who Care About Women's Lives provides male
support for clinics that are picketed by anti-choice activists, sets up information tables, and does lobbying. On
Father's Day, 1989, they held a March for Women's
Lives in San Francisco, and they recently sent a
message to President Bush in the form of 10,000 coat
hangers. They say that they have no interest in debating
anti-choice women, but have a real interest in telling
anti-choice males to "butt out" of an issue that is none
of their business. Men Who Care is composed of men
who are responding to men who don't care about
women's lives. Any financial contribution or volunteer
work will qualify you as a member. Write to:

Men Who Care About Women's Lives
17 Ashton Avenue
San Francisco, CA 94112

Whichever of the above organizations you choose to support, it must be emphasized that, in view of the fact that the United States Supreme Court has essentially tossed the matter of legislating choice back to the states, involvement with a local affiliate of NARAL is now critical. Therefore, when you contact NARAL, be sure to ask to be directed to the affiliate in your state.

Converting the Convertibles

One important goal of pro-choice is to convert the convertibles, and activate the converted; that is, identify those people who are either on the fence or leaning toward choice and may be unaware of the on-going threat of the right-to-life movement. There are several ways you can become involved in this effort:

*   Host a house meeting. Contact your local affiliate of NARAL (or some other similar organization) and ask that a speaker and some literature be provided. Invite as many friends, relatives, and co-workers as you can think of who might be receptive to learning more about the issues.

- If you belong to a local chapter of the AAUW, OWL, or another similar organization (including receptive church groups), make arrangements for a speaker from a local NARAL group, NOW, Planned Parenthood, or some other pro-choice organization to give a presentation to your group.

- Find out what exists in the way of sex-education classes in your local junior high and high schools; if there is nothing, or if what does exist does not provide adequate birth-control information, let the school board know that you believe that providing accurate information to students is the best way to prevent teenage pregnancy, to say nothing of sexually transmitted diseases.

The Power of the Pen

Doing any one of the following will have greater impact than you may imagine:

- When an organizational newsletter or Action Alert advises you to write to a state or federal legislator regarding a particular piece of legislation, do it. While many organizations provide pre-printed post cards, it is more effective if you write a letter or a card, using your own words to express your support for, or opposition to a particular piece of legislation. Legislators *do* pay attention. If you do not know what to say or how to say it, pick up the phone and call your local or national organization and ask for help. It will be gladly given.

Letters should be addressed to your representatives and state senators in care of either the House of Representatives (or Assembly) or the State Senate Office Building, the state capital and the zip code. Most state Alerts will include this information; if not, call a local affiliate of NOW or NARAL.

Letters to United States Representatives and Senators should be addressed as follows:

House Office Building
Washington, D.C. 20515

Senate Office Building
Washington, D.C. 20510

In the matter of federal appointments (to the Supreme Court, for example), it is very important that you write letters to your senators in support of pro-choice nominees and in opposition to anti-choice nominees. Recall that Robert Bork, an anti-choice nominee to the high court, was not confirmed. This attests to the power of letters to legislators. Hundreds of thousands of pro-choice advocates expressed their opposition to their senators. Also recall that, because pro-choice advocates were weary after that struggle, they did not similarly oppose the nomination of Anthony Kennedy. The lesson learned is that pro-choice advocates must oppose the nominations of any anti-choice nominees, no matter how many there may be.

• Write letters to the Letters-to-the-Editor section of your local newspaper. Just a short letter that expresses your pro-choice position may sway someone who is on the fence. At the very least, it will demonstrate support for the issue and serve to educate the public.

• Write letters of appreciation to state and federal legislators who have demonstrated their support for choice. They appreciate hearing from you, and your letters give them the backing to support pro-choice.

• Write letters of appreciation to columnists who express support for choice; on the other hand, write letters expressing the pro-choice position to columnists who are clearly anti-choice.

• Write letters to the Federal Food and Drug Administration in Washington, D.C. urging that they approve the testing of RU 486 on the grounds that this drug is being studied for its effectiveness in treating glaucoma, Cushing's Syndrome, endometriosis, and breast cancer.

• Along these lines, write some letters of support to drug companies likely to produce and market RU 486. For example, Gynopharma, Inc. in Sommerville, New Jersey has expressed this interest. Syntex and Alza, both in Palo Alto, California, may also be likely companies inasmuch as they have been at the forefront in marketing birth control pills.

• Do this today: Write a letter to the President of the United States and tell him how you feel about freedom of choice. Send it to him at:

   The White House
   Washington, DC 20510

• Donate a copy of this book to your local library.

Adopt A Clinic

Birth-control clinics are being attacked from all sides. With cutbacks in state funding, and anti-choice terrorists attempting to force their closure, your local clinic needs all the support it can get.

Since late 1988, for instance, the patients and staff members of clinics have been under attack by a group called Operation Rescue. Reportedly, this is not a formal organization, but somehow, its members coordinate themselves well enough for hundreds of them to appear suddenly on the doorstep of a particular clinic.

Usually, their attacks take place in the early morning, and members of the group attempt to block the entry (and exit) of both patients and staff. Some lie down in their paths, chant, sing hymns, and verbally harass all who seek to enter or leave. Others do what they call "sidewalk counseling," which consists of imploring patients to not "murder" their "babies." They harass not only abortion patients, but people who seek a range of services, including pre-natal care, testing for sexually transmitted diseases, and contraception.

These anti-choice activists justify their tactics in the name of saving the unborn. But after a number of them were arrested and brought to trial after demonstrating at Family Planning Alternatives in Sunnyvale, California, the judge hearing the case disqualified himself because of the bias he had recently acquired. As he put it, he doubted their sincerity because they had prevented people from obtaining that which would truly prevent abortion, namely, contraception.

Furthermore, these demonstrators agitate under the banner of *local* concerned citizens, but in fact, the arrest records of more that 200 of them who trespassed at the Sunnyvale clinic revealed that only *four* were actually residents of the community, with all others having come from other cities and even other states, some from as far away as New Jersey and Oregon. (As an aside, these outsiders have cost the city of Sunnyvale's law enforcement agency some $20,000 per demonstration. Those who have been arrested have been placed in already-crowded jails in the county.)

Pro-choice leaders advocate "adopting a clinic," offering your services as an escort for patients and becoming part of a support group that stands up for choice when anti-choice demonstrators descend.

To find out how you can help, call your local family planning clinic. If you are unaware of what may exist in your community, contact one of the organizations mentioned above or consult the Yellow Pages of your telephone directory.

Make a Political Commitment to Choice

It may seem obvious, especially if you have already decided to indicate your pro-choice positions to your elected officials, that you would make a political commitment to choice. However, there are people who support choice who don't make a commitment to vote that way. When you don't vote choice, you relinquish your leverage as a voter. For example, many people who say they support choice voted for former President Ronald Reagan, and then voted for President George Bush. How seriously could either of these gentlemen have taken the pro-choice position of those who had voted for them?

Remember that a vote for a candidate who is anti-choice, no matter how he or she stands on other issues, turns out to be a vote against choice. And when it comes to casting your vote for legislators, do remember that no matter how they may personally feel about choice, when they cast their legislative ballots, they will be influenced by who they believe got them elected in the first place, or by those they fear might well vote them out of office. So vote choice, and let candidates for all public offices know that you do.

You can go a giant step further by working in the campaigns of pro-choice candidates. To find out who is pro-choice and who isn't, contact a local affiliate of NARAL or Voters for Choice. Then call the candidates' headquarters and offer to:

- Walk a precinct and deliver materials.

- Staff telephone lines.

- Hold an informational meeting in your home.

- Contribute any special skills you may have or services you can provide through your business if you have one.

- Volunteer to help out with voter registration.

- On election day, volunteer to get out the pro-choice vote.

When you work for a candidate because of his or her position on choice, letters expressing your views on the matter carry more weight once he or she is elected because you can begin with, "As someone who worked in your campaign..."

Putting Your Money Where Your Mouth Is

You like hamburgers? Pizza? Well, you need to know that the owner of Carl's Jr. (a fast-food hamburger chain) is a big supporter of the right-to-life movement. The owner of Domino's Pizza contributed $50,000 to a campaign in 1988 for a Michigan referendum to eliminate state funding of abortions and $30,000 to Operation Rescue in California.

You can put your money where your mouth is, quite literally, by refusing to patronize both of these establishments. You can go a step further by telling them why you're going to get your hamburger at McDonald's and your pizza at Pizza Hut. And you can go even further when you persuade all of your friends to boycott establishments that support anti-choice organizations.

Image Counts

Whether your expression of support for choice comes in the form of a letter, campaigning for a pro-choice candidate, or participating in a demonstration to show support for the issue or a clinic, remember that image counts. Letters should be simple and to the point and never abusive. If you choose to stand up and be counted in a group supporting a clinic, dress nicely, be orderly, and, if you carry a sign to express your convictions, keep it simple and non-derogatory. If you choose to work for a candidate, all of the above applies because you must represent him or her to potential voters in the best possible light. Always remember that a greater world may be watching and that your goal is to protect freedom of choice.

A Final Word

To be effective in preserving choice, we must always remember that winning one battle, or even winning one after another, is not the same as winning the war, because the war will *never* be over. Vigilance is the price we must pay to maintain past gains and deter efforts to deny our freedoms.

Even if getting an abortion has never been on one's agenda, how can anyone second guess the motives of women so driven? The reasons given for terminating a pregnancy may sometimes seem superficial to the casual observer, but who really knows what they may be for many women? To borrow the words of Margaret Sanger, their reasons are probably "as vast as the sky," as is their determination. The matter of choice, thus, is best left to the people involved. Put simply, it is nobody else's business.

Our business, then, is to keep it that way. It doesn't matter whether the efforts each of us make are large or small, but that we all do what we can to preserve choice. To paraphrase Edmund Burke, nobody ever made a greater mistake than those who did nothing because they could do only a little.

So, whatever it is, do it.

Bibliography

Annas, George J. *"Webster* and the Politics of Abortion." *Hastings Center Report*, March/April 1989.

Associated Press. "Abortion Activists Battle Over 'Morning After' Pill." Washington, D.C., June 2, 1989.

CDRR News, July/August 1988.

Cisler, Lucinda. "Unfinished Business: Birth Control and Women's Liberation." *Sisterhood is Powerful*, ed. Robin Morgan. New York: Vintage, 1970.

Conway, Flo, and Siegelman, Jim. *Holy Terror*. New York: Delta, 1984.

Crawford, Alan. *Thunder on the Right*. New York: Pantheon, 1980.

Crawford, Christina. "Conspiracy of Silence," *Ladies' Home Journal*, November 1981.

Dezell, Maureen, "RU 486," *Boston Globe*, March 17, 1989.

Doerr, Edd, and James W. Prescott. *Abortion Rights and Fetal 'Personhood.'* Long Beach, CA: Centerline Press, 1989.

Ellingston, Jenefer. *We Are the Mainstream*. Catholics for a Free Choice, 1981.

Ehrlich, Anne H. and Paul R. "Population and Development Misunderstood," *The Amicus Journal*, Summer 1986.

Ehrlich, Paul. "Humankind's War Against Homo Sapiens," *Defenders*, Nov/Dec 85.

Faux, Marian. *Roe v. Wade: The Untold Story of the Landmark Supreme Court Decision That Made Abortion Legal.* New York: Macmillan, 1988; New American Library, 1989.

Fontana, Vincent, M.D. *Somewhere a Child is Crying.* New York: Macmillan, 1973.

Fraser, Laura. "Pill Politics," *Mother Jones*, June 1988.

Gallup, George, Jr., and Gallup, Alec. "Most Oppose Reversal of Abortion-Rights Case," *San Francisco Chronicle*, January 22, 1989.

Greenhouse, Linda, "Change in Course," *New York Times*, July 4, 1989.

Greenhouse, Steven. "The Uphill Battle to Market the French Abortion Pill," *San Francisco Chronicle, This World*, February 26, 1989.

Gregory, Hamilton, ed. *The Religious Case for Abortion.* Detroit: Madison & Polk, 1983.

Harvey, Brett. "The Morning After," *Mother Jones*, May 1989.

Howe, Louise Kapp. *Moments on Maple Avenue: The Reality of Abortion.* New York: Macmillan, 1984.

Hurst, Jane. *The History of Abortion in the Catholic Church.* Catholics for a Free Choice, 1981.

International Dateline, Population Communications International, April 1989.

Jacobson, Jodi L. "Choice at any Cost," *World Watch*, March-April 1988.

Jones, Landon Y. *Great Expectations.* New York: Ballantine, 1980.

Kohn, Richard. *The Church in a Democracy.* Catholics for a Free Choice, 1981.

Krascoff, Dalia. "Back-Street Abortion: A Woman's Story," *San Jose Mercury News,* January 22, 1989.

Lader, Lawrence. *Abortion.* Indianapolis: Bobbs-Merrill, 1966.

Levin, Beatrice. *Women and Medicine.* Metuchin, NJ: The Scarecrow Press, Inc., 1980; specifically Chapter 18, "Abortion and the Abused Child.".

Liner, Robert. "Letters," *San Francisco Chronicle,* March 3, 1989.

Luker, Kristin. *Abortion and the Politics of Motherhood.* Berkeley: University of California Press, 1984.

Martin, Nina. "Abortion Clinics Brace for Ruling by High Court," *San Francisco Examiner,* June 25, 1989.

Mathews, Jay. "Her Abortion was Judged by the World," *Washington Post* and *San Jose Mercury News,* May 21, 1987.

Matulis, Sherry. "Abortion 1954," in *The Religious Case for Abortion,* ed. Hamilton Gregory. Detroit: Madison & Polk, 1983.

Merton, Andrew H. *Enemies of Choice.* Boston: Beacon Press, 1981.

Mohr, James. *Abortion in America: The Origins and Evolution of National Policy, 1800-1900.* New York: Oxford University Press, 1978.

Mumford, Stephen D. *American Democracy & the Vatican: Population Growth & National Security.*

Amherst, NY: The Humanist Press, 1984. See also *The Pope and the New Apocalypse: The Holy War Against Family Planning.* North Carolina: Center for Research on Population and National Security, 1986.

New York Times, July 4, 1989.

Newsweek. "Abortion in the Form of a Pill," April 17, 1989.

Noonan, John T. *Contraception.* Cambridge, Mass: Harvard University Press, 1965. Also, *A Private Choice: Abortion in America in the Seventies.* New York: Free Press, 1979.

Ornstein, Robert, and Ehrlich, Paul. *New World New Mind.* New York: Doubleday, 1989.

Paige, Connie. *The Right to Lifers.* New York: Summit Books, 1983.

Potts, Malcolm, M.D. "The Uncertain Journey." *Science '82*, March 1982.

Rader, Dotson. "Who Will Help the Children." *Parade*, September 5, 1982.

Radl, Shirley Rogers. *The Invisible Woman: Target of the Religious New Right.* New York: Delta/Merloyd Lawrence, 1983. Also *Mother's Day is Over.* New York: Arbor House, 1987.

RCAR Options, Vol. 15, No. 2, Winter 1988.

Robertson, Constance. "Thank God for Legal Abortion," in *The Religious Case for Abortion*, ed., Hamilton Gregory. Asheville, North Carolina: Madison & Polk, 1983.

Rowan, Carl, *Dallas Morning News*, July 5, 1989.

Sanger, Margaret. *Margaret Sanger: An Autobiography*. New York: W.W. Norton & Company, 1938; Dover Publications, 1971.

Skowronski, Margery. *Abortion and Alternatives*. Millbrae, CA: Les Femmes, 1977.

Spurgeon, Graham. "Is Abortion Murder," in *The Religious Case for Abortion*, Ed., Hamilton Gregory. Asheville, North Carolina: Madison & Polk, 1983.

Stanley, Autumn. *Mothers of Invention*. Metuchin, NJ: Scarecrow Press, in press.

Steinem, Gloria. "The Nazi Connection," in *Speak Out*, ed. Herbert F. Vetter. Boston: Beacon Press, 1982.

Suh, Mary. "RU Detour," *Ms.*, January/February 1989.

Workman, Diana. "Planned Parenthood/Pro-Choice," *Political Woman*, Summer 1986.

Zimmerman, David R. "Abortion Clinics' Toughest Cases," *Medical World News*, March 9, 1987.

ZPG National Reporter, August 1970.

About the Author

Shirley L. Radl is the author of several books about women's issues and parenting, including *Mother's Day Is Over*, *The Mother's Survival Guide*, *The Invisible Woman*, and, with Dr. Philip G. Zimbardo, *The Shy Child*. A mother of two children, she has also written articles on parenting for *American Baby*, *The Ladies' Home Journal*, and *Family Circle*. Over the years, she has been involved in organizations dedicated to important social issues, having served as executive director for Zero Population Growth and founder of the Parental Stress Hotline in Palo Alto, California. She currently serves as a consultant to the California Pro-Choice Education Fund and is Chair of the Board of Family Planning Alternatives, a birth-control clinic in Sunnyvale, California. Her commitment to every aspect of family planning stems from her deep concern over women's rights and an equally deep concern over the health and welfare of children the world over.